MINNESOTA CRAFT BREWERS GUILD

MINNESOTA BREWERS COOKBOOK

RECIPES BY BREWERIES/BREWPUBS FOR CRAFT BEER FANS

MINNESOTA BREWERS COOKBOOK

Copyright © 2020 by The Minnesota Craft Brewers Guild

807 Broadway St. NE, Ste 14
Minneapolis, MN 55413
www.mncraftbrew.org

All rights reserved. No part of this book may be reproduced or transmitted in any form or by any means without written permission from the author.

Design by Lauren Bennett McGinty / MNCBG Staff

ISBN 978-0-578-24245-3

Printed in USA by 48HrBooks (www.48HrBooks.com)

About The Minnesota Craft Brewers Guild

In 2000, a small group of brewers founded The Minnesota Craft Brewers Guild, a 501(c)(6) nonprofit association, to help support a growing industry. Twenty years later, the number of Minnesota craft breweries and brewpubs has blossomed into more than 200 small, independent businesses with more than 4,500 employees.

Our mission is to promote, protect, and grow a robust Minnesota craft brewing industry by building a healthy beer culture and community that allows for independent brewers, industry stakeholders, and craft beer fans to thrive.

We are proud to support our more than 160 member breweries and brewpubs through festivals like Winterfest, All Pints North, and Autumn Brew Review; the "Brewed in Minnesota" exhibit at the Minnesota State Fair; ongoing educational resources and events; and federal and state advocacy.

We couldn't do any of this without our thousands of craft beer fans. Proceeds from this book support our mission and the services we provide to the Minnesota craft beer industry. So from all of us at the Guild, thank you for supporting Minnesota craft beer—cheers!

How This Book Is Organized

First and foremost, this is a book about **BEER**.

These unique recipes were developed to call attention to the special flavors of your favorite craft beers. To highlight those flavors, we've organized this book by beer categories rather than ingredient or meal type.

Got a few pilsners in the fridge? Flip to the Crisp & Clean section and find recipes for any occasion. Have a sour that you've been wanting to try? Check out the Fruity, Spicy, Tart & Funky category to see what you can whip up.

Most recipes in this book utilize a specific brand of beer, but many provide substitutions to make the dish work for your tastes (or what you have on hand). As long as you use a beer in that flavor category, you'll see some excellent results made with local beer and a lot of love.

Each section features information about the beer category including what beers fit in that category and what foods pair well with the beer.

These recipes are all about working with fresh, local brews, so don't be shy. Try something new and share your results with friends and family.

CONTENTS

CRISP & CLEAN 8

- Duck Fat Chicken "Carnitas"
- IGB Chili
- Beer-Battered Walleye Sandwich
- Asparagus Risotto
- Pragmatic Pils Lime Shrimp
- Jeff Zierdt's Tater Tot Hotdish
- North Shore Fish Fry
- Carrot Cake a la Tanzenwald

DARK & ROASTY 20

- Happy Wife Bacon Jam
- Loopy Beef Sandwich
- Birch's Baby Back Ribs
- PB & BBQ
- Browncoat Risotto with Beef Short Ribs
- Honey Porter Braised Short Rib Cottage Pie
- BAMF'D Tri-Tip
- Town Hall Shepherds Pie
- Chocolate Stout Cake
- Peanut Butter Apple Crumble
- Lift Bridge Stout Brownies
- Stoneware Stout Chocolate Cake

FRUITY, SPICY, TART & FUNKY 38

- Kieran's Rhubarb Gold Cuban Sandwich
- Wild Mushroom Pasta
- Kriek Braised and Glazed Beef Short Ribs
- Popper Ribs

HOPPY & BITTER 45

- Spiral Into This Cheese Dip
- Hot Dog Roller Level-Up
- Excelsior BrewGrub Salmon Cake Sliders
- Dark Lager Beef Stacker

MALTY & SWEET 53

- Beer-Battered Shrimp
- Campfire 14° ESB Philly Cheesesteak
- Ursa Minor Brewing Pizza Dough
- Brewhall Pizza
- Mussels de Belgique
- Amber Pot Pie
- Truth Be Told Pork Belly
- Coq au Bier
- Trails Giving Turkey
- Wee Heavy Creme Brulee
- Sticky Toffee Pudding
- Peanut Butter Stout Pudding
- Vanilla Latte Caramel Cream

PHOTO CREDITS 72
THANK YOU 73
BREWERY MAP 78
INDEX 82

Crisp & Clean

Crisp & Clean beers include anything that is light, fresh, and easy-drinking. The category includes pilsners, kölsches, cream ales, blonde ales, and more.

When pairing food and drink, Crisp & Clean beers go great with salty and acidic foods because they can cleanse the palate and balance the intensity of the food.

These beers are often enjoyed with pretzels, cheese and olive plates, or chips, but the following recipes will give you even more possibilities!

When cooking with beer, the light flavors of a delicate lager or ale can blend well with so many foods. The following recipes, everything from tomatillo salsa to carrot cake, give you a chance to experience the range that a Crisp & Clean beer may offer.

Duck Fat Chicken "Carnitas" 9
Eastlake Craft Brewery

IGB Chili 11
Inver Grove Brewing Company

Beer-Battered Walleye Sandwich 12
GLUEK BEER

Asparagus Risotto 13
Klockow Brewing Company

Pragmatic Pils Lime Shrimp 14
Pryes Brewing Company

Jeff Zierdt's Tater Tot Hotdish 16
Lupulin Brewing Company

North Shore Fish Fry 17
Castle Danger Brewery

Carrot Cake a la Tanzenwald 18
Tanzenwald Brewing Company

Duck Fat Chicken "Carnitas" with Beer Tomatillo Salsa

SUBMITTED BY: RYAN PITMAN, FOUNDER / HEAD BREWER—EASTLAKE CRAFT BREWERY, MINNEAPOLIS

This recipe is how Eastlake Craft Brewery makes carnitas without pork.

Adjust the quantities for serving:

- chicken thighs or Brussels sprouts
- duck fat or coconut oil
- enough garlic to choke a horse
- onion, chopped
- jalapeño
- fresh squeezed orange juice
- fresh squeezed lime juice
- cumin
- chili powder
- salt
- bunch of tomatillos
- Southside Pils
- queso fresco
- cilantro
- tortillas

MAKES HOWEVER MANY YOU WANT

1. Marinate your chicken or sprouts in a mixture of OJ, Pils, lime juice, the spices, jalapeño, and smashed garlic for a day or two.
2. Slow-cook in the marinade (crock pot for 8 hours or braising for a few hours is great for this).
3. Separate the meat/sprouts from the liquid. Collect any fat that collects on top of the liquid and mix into the chicken/sprouts.
4. Quarter the tomatillos and put them in the marinade liquid for a few minutes. Simmering wouldn't hurt.
5. Puree tomatillos and marinade for salsa.
6. Meanwhile, take the shredded chicken or sprouts, and add a TON of duck fat or coconut oil (seriously, like a ton) and toss it under a broiler or on a grill until it's as crispy as you like.
7. Add filling to tortilla and top with chopped fresh onions, cilantro, and queso fresco

BEER PAIRING: Pilsner, light beer, lime sour

Photo: Page 10, top

IGB Chili

SUBMITTED BY: GLEN BRUESTLE, HEAD CHEF/COOKIE—INVER GROVE BREWING COMPANY, INVER GROVE HEIGHTS

Glen came up with this recipe after tasting the first batch of house-made salsa and Bloody Mary mix. The inspiration was drawn from the spice of the Bloody Mary mix and the oven-roasted flavor from the IGB house salsa. Glen really wanted a simple comfort food that could warm guests on a cold MN winter day.

1 lb	ground beef
1/2 c	onion, chopped
1/2 c	red pepper, chopped
2 tsp	garlic, chopped
1	whole jalepeño, chopped
2 tsp	garlic powder
1 tbsp	cocoa powder
1 tbsp	brown sugar
2 tbsp	chili powder
4 tsp	salt
3 c	of IGB Bloody Mary Mix (or other)
3 c	of IGB salsa (or other)
1 c	chicken stock (optional)
1	can black beans
1	can kidney beans

SERVES 4-6

1. In large soup pot, add ground beef, onions, red pepper, chopped garlic, and jalapeño. Cook for 6–7 minutes while breaking apart the beef with a wooden spoon.
2. Add the rest of the dry ingredients, stir until well combined.
3. Stir in bloody mix, salsa, chicken stock, black beans, and kidney beans, then simmer for 20–25 minutes.
4. Remove from heat, and let the chili rest for about 10 minutes.
5. Top chili with cojita cheese and crema (or your favorite toppings) and serve with tortilla chips.

BEER PAIRING: *Knee High American Cream Ale*

Photos: Page 10, bottom left & right

Beer-Battered Walleye Sandwich

SUBMITTED BY: LINDA RAE HOLCOMB, PRESIDENT—GLUEK BEER, MINNEAPOLIS

This award-winning walleye sandwich has been a best seller at Gluek's Bar & Restaurant for decades. It tastes great using either the GLUEK PILSENER or GLUEK CREAM ALE and obviously tastes better with a cold beer! Cheers!

2 c	flour
1 1/2 tsp	salt
1/2 tsp	black pepper
1/2 tsp	garlic powder
1/2 tsp	lemon pepper
dash	paprika
2	eggs, beaten
4	walleye fillets
1/2 c	GLUEK BEER
2-3 tbsp	butter or cooking oil
	lemon and/or garnish of choice

MAKES 4

1. Combine dry fish batter ingredients in a shallow bowl and set aside.
2. Beat the eggs and add 1/2 cup GLUEK BEER, mix gently.
3. Take each walleye fillet and dip both sides in the GLUEK BEER egg wash, then dredge each fillet in the dry mix, coating the fillet thoroughly.
4. Heat pan to medium and add the butter or cooking oil, then fry the fillet until it's golden brown on both sides.
5. Garnish with a lemon wedge or create a GLUEK BEER battered walleye sandwich!

BEER PAIRING: GLUEK BOHEMIAN PILSENER or GLUEK CREAM ALE

Photo: Page 15, top

GLUEK BEER was established on the banks of the Mississippi River in 1857, one year before Minnesota was officially declared a state. All Gluek Beer is gluten-removed and is of the highest quality standard.

Asparagus Risotto

SUBMITTED BY: TASHA KLOCKOW, OWNER & MANAGER—
KLOCKOW BREWING COMPANY, GRAND RAPIDS

Tasha loves to make comfort food for her family and friends. This creamy risotto with crunchy asparagus fits the bill perfectly because it is cozy and warming, yet bright and flavorful.

6 c	broth (or 4 c broth & 2 c water)
5 tbsp	unsalted butter
1	large onion, chopped fine
1 lb	pound asparagus; cut to desired length, ends reserved for broth
to taste	salt & pepper
2-4	garlic cloves, minced
2 c	Arborio rice
1 c	Crosswind Kölsch, or any other dry, light beer
1/2 c	frozen peas
1 c	grated Parmesan
1/2–1	lemon

SERVES 4–6

1. Put 6 cups broth into a pot and bring pot to a boil.
2. Prep the onion and cut off the asparagus ends. Add the scraps into the large pot to add extra flavor to the broth. Cover and reduce heat to a simmer.
3. In a large pan over medium heat, melt 2 tablespoons butter. Add onion and a pinch of salt, cook until soft, about 5 minutes. Add garlic and cook until fragrant, about 30 seconds. Add the rice, stirring constantly for about 3 minutes, until the edges of the grains start to turn translucent.
4. While stirring, add 1 cup of dry, light beer, until all the liquid is absorbed; about 2 minutes.
5. Using a strainer, carefully pour 5 cups of the hot broth into a measuring cup. Add broth to the rice. Reduce heat to medium-low, cover and cook for 18 minutes, stirring every 6 minutes. Add more broth if it absorbs too quickly.
6. With 6 minutes left, melt 1 tablespoon of butter in a pan and add the asparagus, cook for about 5 minutes; do not overcook, it should be crunchy! Add peas and cook for 1 minute.
7. Remove peas and asparagus from heat.
8. Add 1/2 cup more of the hot broth to rice and stir constantly, consistency should be creamy. Add Parmesan and stir until combined. Remove from heat and cover for 5 minutes.
9. Stir in remaining 2 tablespoons of butter and juice 1/2–1 lemon to taste. Fold in asparagus and peas and add salt and pepper to taste.
10. Serve! Prost!

BEER PAIRING: *Crosswind Kölsch, or whatever beer it was cooked with*

Photos: Page 15, middle left & right

Pragmatic Pils Lime Shrimp

SUBMITTED BY: JEREMY PRYES, HEAD BREWER—PRYES BREWING COMPANY, MINNEAPOLIS

Jeremy loves preparing this light, bright, citrusy seafood dish. It's well balanced, marginally spicy, and keeps the focus on the star of the dish—shrimp—while pairing beautifully with a Pryes Pragmatic Pils to mingle with the lime and cut through the lingering jalapeño heat. Note: Serve with rice, and make it prior to cooking the listed ingredients—this meal only takes a moment to complete.

1 c	cooked rice
2 tbsp	olive oil
5	shallots, chopped
2	cloves garlic, chopped
1/4	jalepeño, chopped
1 tsp	cumin
1 lb	shrimp, peeled & deveined
1/4 c	Pryes Pragmatic Pils
1/4 c	lime juice (approx. 2 big limes)
1 tsp	lime zest
	salt & pepper
1/4 c	cilantro, chopped
	cilantro
	sliced limes

SERVES 2-4

1. Heat the oil in a pan. Add the garlic, jalapeño, and cumin and sauté until fragrant, about 1 minute.
2. Add Pryes Pragmatic Pils and stir in for 1 minute.
3. Add the shrimp and cook until the shrimp are pink, about 1–3 minutes per side. Zest limes on top of the shrimp on second side, and juice both limes on top of shrimp.
4. Add chopped shallots and cilantro to pan and stir for 30 seconds. Salt and pepper to taste and remove from the heat.
5. Lay bed of rice on plate and place shrimp on top of rice. Ladle broth from pan over shrimp and rice.
6. Garnish with cilantro and sliced limes. Pour the rest of the Pryes Pragmatic Pils in a glass and enjoy!

BEER PAIRING: Pryes Pragmatic Pils

Photos: Page 15, bottom left & right

Jeff Zierdt's Tater Tot Hotdish

SUBMITTED BY: JEFF ZIERDT, CO-FOUNDER & PRESIDENT—LUPULIN BREWING, BIG LAKE

Hotdish or casserole? That is the question...it's a hotdish, full stop. Jeff's Tater Tot Hotdish, a spin on a classic MN comfort food, is a brewery favorite. It goes deeper though... If you get a chance, ask him about his tater tot conspiracy theory...

1 1/2 lbs	ground beef
1 c	diced onion
1 pinch	garlic powder, or to taste
1 pinch	salt & pepper or to taste
28 oz	package frozen mixed vegetables
26 1/2 oz	can condensed cream of mushroom soup
28 oz	package frozen tater tots (may replace with other veggie tots)
2 c	shredded cheddar cheese
1 pinch	paprika
1 pinch	dried parsley flakes, or to taste

SERVES 6–8

1. Preheat oven to 350° F. Grease a 9x13-inch baking dish.
2. Cook and stir ground beef, onion, garlic powder, salt, and black pepper in a skillet over medium heat until beef is browned and crumbly, 7–10 minutes. Drain.
3. Spread beef mixture into the bottom of the prepared baking dish and spread bag of frozen mixed vegetables over the top of the beef mixture.
4. Stir cream of mushroom soup, tater tots, and cheddar cheese together in a large bowl until your tots are evenly coated in soup and cheese.
5. Spread tater tot mixture over beef mixture.
6. Bake in preheated oven until browned and bubbling, or about 45–60 minutes depending on your oven.
7. Remove from oven, sprinkle paprika and parsley flakes over the top, and serve!

BEER PAIRING: Belgian Blonde Ale, Dortmunder Lager, Festbier

Photo: Page 19, top

North Shore Fish Fry

SUBMITTED BY: JAMIE MACFARLANE, CO-FOUNDER AND CFO—
CASTLE DANGER BREWERY, TWO HARBORS

Jamie created this dangerously good fish fry recipe over the years. She found that North Shore Lager works the best, but Castle Cream Ale can be used in a pinch. Nothing says "you're on the North Shore" like a fresh beer-battered fish fry.

	flour
1	egg
1/2	can North Shore Lager
	saltine crackers, crushed fine
	fish fillets, Lake Superior herring recommended
4 c	canola oil
to taste	kosher salt

MAKES 4-6

1. In a large pot or deep fryer, add oil. Using a thermometer, heat oil to 350° F.
2. Get three large plates or shallow bowls. In one, add flour. In the middle, add the egg and beer; whisk to combine. In the third, add the crushed saltines.
3. Dredge fish in flour, then beer mix, then crackers.
4. Carefully lower into oil. Add more fillets as space allows. Flip fish over half way, if needed.
5. When golden brown and cooked, remove to paper towel-lined tray. Immediately sprinkle with kosher salt.

BEER PAIRING: North Shore Lager or Castle Cream Ale

Photos: Page 19, middle left & right

Jamie and Clint MacFarlane founded Castle Danger Brewery in 2011 (now joined by co-owners Lon and Mandy Larson). Jamie is quite the cook and baker, treating brewery employees to birthday treats and her family to nightly home-cooked meals. The Castle Danger Fish Fry is one of Jamie's family's recipes. Her grandfather, Mark Lind, was a commercial fisherman on Lake Superior for his entire life. In the Lind family, this was the only way to cook fresh-caught fish.

Carrot Cake a la Tanzenwald

SUBMITTED BY: LUC GUERBER, TANZENWALD'S ORIGINAL PASTRY CHEF/BREWER'S APPRENTICE—TANZENWALD BREWING COMPANY, NORTHFIELD

This carrot cake features an exotic blend of freshly ground cardamom, grated ginger, and a whole orange, including the pulp and zest. There is a generous portion of cream cheese frosting in every glorious bite. You won't be missing the raisins that are traditionally in a carrot cake, and this recipe omits walnuts to be nut-allergy friendly, so even more people can enjoy this one-of-a-kind taste sensation.

Cake Batter:

1	whole orange (pureed with zest & pith)
5	eggs
1 c	canola or vegetable oil
2 c	flour
2 c	brown sugar
1 tbsp	baking soda
1 tbsp	baking powder
1 1/2 tbsp	cardamom
1/2 tsp	salt
12 1/2-13 oz	peeled, grated carrots (approx. 2 cups)
2 1/2 oz	grated or minced ginger

Frosting:

24 oz	cream cheese, room temp
1 c	unsalted butter, room temp (2 sticks)
1 tbsp	vanilla extract
6 c	powdered sugar (more may be needed to thicken)

SERVES 8–12

1. Preheat oven to 350° F. Grease and flour three 9-inch round baking pans.
2. Whip pureed orange and eggs until fluffy, drizzle oil into while whipping.
3. Whisk together all dry ingredients. Gradually add dry ingredient mixture to orange & egg puree, beat on medium speed until just combined, scraping down the bowl at least once to be sure everything is well mixed.
4. Fold grated carrots and ginger into batter by hand.
5. Pour the batter evenly into the prepared cake pans and bake for 25–30 minutes total. Depending on your oven, you may need rotate pans halfway through. Cool on a rack(s) to room temperature.
6. While the cake is baking, mix your frosting. Cream the cream cheese and butter together with a mixer on medium speed. Once combined, add vanilla; mix thoroughly. Add powdered sugar 1 cup at a time, fully incorporating between cups. More powdered sugar may be required if the frosting is not thick enough.
7. Once the cake layers are cool, use a large knife to level off the domed tops of the cake so they are level and even.
8. Frost each layer with cream cheese frosting, stack cakes, and frost the outside.
9. Top with additional finely grated carrots or decorate as desired.

BEER PAIRING: *Tanzenwald's Guns-A-Blazin Double IPA, or any West Coast-style IPA*

Photo: Page 19, bottom

Dark & Roasty

Featuring Russian imperial stouts, porters, coffee stouts, and more, the Dark & Roasty category is bold and robust.

The intensity of chocolate, caramel, coffee, peanut butter, and other flavors in these beers can vary dramatically. These flavors are only matched by the deep roasted malt that gives the beer a rich warm character.

No matter what Dark & Roasty beer you choose to enjoy, it will pair beautifully with rich, sweet, and nutty foods like cheeses, roasted vegetables, and sweet BBQ. It's no surprise that these beers pair well with desserts too—who hasn't had a nice chocolaty stout and imagined pouring it over cold ice cream?

Happy Wife Bacon Jam 21
Three Twenty Brewing Co.

Loopy Beef Sandwich 23
Fulton Brewing Company

Birch's Baby Back Ribs 24
Birch's On The Lake

PB & BBQ 25
Inbound BrewCo

Browncoat Risotto with Beef Short Rib 27
LTS Brewing Company

Honey Porter Braised Short Rib Cottage Pie 28
Forgotten Star Brewing Company

BAMF'D Tri-Tip 30
HeadFlyer Brewing

Town Hall Shepherds Pie 31
Town Hall Brewery

Chocolate Stout Cake 33
Back Channel Brewing

Peanut Butter Apple Crumble 34
Dangerous Man Brewing

Lift Bridge Stout Brownies 35
Lift Bridge Brewery

Stoneware Stout Chocolate Cake 37
Red Wing Brewery

Happy Wife Bacon Jam

SUBMITTED BY: THREE TWENTY BREWING CO., PINE CITY, WITH TIM & SHANNON KARNICK—OWNERS OF TIKI TIM'S FOOD TRUCK AND THE FORT RESTAURANT, NORTH BRANCH

Tim and Shannon use this recipe to create Three Twenty Brewing Co's bacon jam burger, which-topped with the bacon jam, goat cheese, and arugula. As an alternative, they suggest adding it to your favorite charcuterie board!

1 lb	bacon, cut into 1" pieces
1	large red onion, chopped
3	gloves garlic, minced
1 c	Three Twenty Happy Wife Porter
1/3 c	balsamic vinegar
1/3 c	dark brown sugar
1/4 c	pure maple syrup
dash	salt

MAKES 1 1/2 CUPS

1. In a medium saucepan over medium heat, cook bacon until crispy. Transfer cooked bacon to a paper towel-lined plate.
2. Reserve 2 tablespoons of bacon grease in the pan and caramelize the onions in the bacon grease. Add the garlic to onions and stir for one minute.
3. Stir in Happy Wife Porter, balsamic vinegar, dark brown sugar, maple syrup and salt. Simmer over medium heat until the liquid has reduced and the onions are jammy.
4. Let cool, then transfer to a food processor along with the bacon and pulse until desired consistency. Store in a mason jar in the fridge for up to a week or freeze for up to 3 months.
5. Top a burger with the jam, goat cheese and arugula, or add to your favorite charcuterie board!

BEER PAIRING: Three Twenty Happy Wife Porter

Photo: Page 22, top

Three Twenty's Happy Wife Porter won first place in the Porter Category and third overall at the 2019 Minnesota Craft Brewers Guild Brewers Cup! Pictured here are founders Nick & Cassandra Olson at the 2019 awards ceremony.

Loopy Beef Sandwich

SUBMITTED BY: FULTON BREWING COMPANY, MINNEAPOLIS, WITH BRENT HANSON, HEAD CHEF OF THE FULTON TAPROOM KITCHEN

Chef Brent designed this recipe for the taproom kitchen to pair perfectly with (and be cooked with) Fulton Proper Porter.

Loopy Beef:

- 3-4 lb beef chuck roast
- 2-3 tbsp oil
- 3 limes, juiced
- 1 can chipotle in adobo sauce
- 7 cloves garlic
- 1 1/2 tbsp cumin
- 1 1/2 tbsp oregano
- 6 bay leaves
- 6 oz Proper Porter
- 1/3 c apple cider vinegar

Chimichurri:

- 1/2 c parsley, chopped
- 1/4 c red wine vinegar
- 6 cloves garlic, minced
- 3 tbsp chopped fresh oregano
- 3 tbsp crushed red pepper flakes
- 3/4 c olive oil
- salt & pepper

Fixings:

- French rolls
- shredded romaine lettuce
- guacamole
- sliced onion (red or white)
- cotija cheese

SERVES 6–8

1. Preheat the oven to 185° F.
2. Salt and pepper the beef roast, brown on all sides in oil, and transfer to a roasting pan.
3. Process the remaining Loopy Beef ingredients in a blender, pour over the browned beef, and cover in foil.
4. Braise in the oven, covered, for about 6 hours.
5. Uncover, shred the roast, and return to the oven for 30 minutes to crisp up a bit (or broil for about 5 minutes).
6. Chop all herbs (fine or rough, depending on your liking).
7. Mix chimichurri ingredients and let rest for 30 minutes for flavors to combine. This can be made ahead of time and refrigerated, just let it come back to room temp before using.
8. Slice the French roll, cover the bottom with a layer of lettuce, and dress the lettuce with chimichurri.
9. Layer the loopy beef on top of the dressed lettuce, and top with sliced onion and cotija cheese.
10. Schmear the top of the roll with guacamole, toss it on top, and cut in half, on a bias.
11. Open a Fulton Porter or Stout to pair, and enjoy! (The chef can confirm that a Stout or Porter from another wonderful MN Brewery pairs fantastically as well.)

Alternative Cooking Methods:

Crockpot: Cook on low in crock pot for 6–8 hours, and then crisp in oven.

Sous vide: Cook at 185° for 6–8 hours, and then crisp in the oven.

BEER PAIRING: Fulton Proper Porter, Chocolate Oatmeal Stout, Worthy Adversary Imperial Stout, or War and Peace Imperial Coffee Stout

Photo: Page 22, bottom

Birch's Baby Back Ribs

SUBMITTED BY: BIRCH'S ON THE LAKE, LONG LAKE, WITH CHEF JON BOETEL & BURT JOSEPH

Birch's on the Lake's famous baby back ribs, which they've had available since they opened in 2015, are always a customer favorite.

Rib Rub:

2	slabs baby back ribs
1 tsp	black pepper
1 tsp	paprika
2 tsp	kosher salt
2 tsp	brown sugar
1/2 tsp	dry mustard
2 tsp	chili powder
1/2 tsp	celery seed
1 tsp	garlic powder
1 tsp	onion powder
1/2 tsp	oregano powder

Birch's BBQ Sauce:

2 c	ketchup
1/2 c	water
1/2 c	onion, grated
1 tbsp	garlic salt
3 tbsp	rib rub
2 tsp	yellow mustard
2 tbsp	Frank's Red hot sauce
2 tbsp	lemon juice
1/4 c	honey
1 tsp	liquid smoke (optional)

SERVES 6-8

Prepare the Ribs:
1. Mix all rib rub ingredients together in a bowl.
2. Add all sauce ingredients (including a portion of the rib rub) to a sauce pot and simmer for 45–60 minutes.
3. Cover your ribs with the remaining dry rub.

For Smoker:
1. Preheat your smoker to 200° F.
2. Place ribs on upper grate and slow smoke 1 hour; remove.
3. Wrap in foil and return to smoker at 200° F and cook additional 2 hours until ribs are tender.

For Oven and Grill:
1. Preheat oven to 350° F.
2. Cover the dish tightly with aluminum foil and bake until the meat begins to pull away from the ends of the bones and the ribs are just tender, about 1 1/2 hours. You can bake the ribs up to a day before and keep them refrigerated. Bring refrigerated ribs to room temperature about 1 hour before you grill them.
3. Preheat an outdoor grill to medium-high heat.
4. Grill the ribs, flip, then brush them with the sauce, until they're crispy and heated through, about 10 minutes. Move the ribs around as they grill; the sugar in barbecue sauce makes it easy for them to burn.

BEER PAIRING: Birch's Vanilla Milk Stout, or any stout or porter

Photo: Page 26, top

PB & BBQ

SUBMITTED BY: INBOUND BREWCO, MINNEAPOLIS, AND CHEF/OWNER SAUL OF ORALE MEXICAN EATS

Produced in collaboration with Inbound BrewCo and Orale Mexican Eats, PB & BBQ features polenta and beer-braised ribs served with BBQ sauce made with Contains Nuts Peanut Butter Milk Stout.

Stout Beer BBQ Sauce:

- 1 1/2 cans peanut butter milk stout beer (16 oz cans)
- 1/3 c brown sugar
- 1/4 c rice wine vinegar
- 3 tsp soy sauce
- 1/2 c molasses
- 2 tsp spicy mustard
- 1/4 c onion powder
- 1/4 c garlic powder
- 1 tsp paprika
- 2 tsp honey
- 1/2 c ketchup
- 6 oz tomato paste
- 10 oz crushed tomatoes
- 1/4 c chipotle in adobo
- 1 tbsp Worcestershire sauce

Braised BBQ Short Ribs:

- 2 lbs beef short ribs (English cut)
- 1 tbsp salt
- 1 tbsp black pepper
- 3 cloves garlic, crushed
- 1/2 medium red onion
- 1/2 can peanut butter stout beer (16 oz can)
- 2 c Stout Beer BBQ Sauce

SERVES 2–4

1. Add beer to a pot and bring to a boil.
2. Turn down the heat to medium to low, add all the other BBQ sauce ingredients in the pot. Let it simmer for 15 minutes, stirring frequently so it does not stick or burn on the bottom.
3. Turn the heat off and let it sit to cool down.
4. Pat dry the short ribs and rub with salt and pepper.
5. In an oven-safe pan on the stove, sear the short ribs on all sides.
6. Remove short ribs from the pan, then caramelize red onions in the same pan for about 30 seconds. Add garlic, then turn the heat off.
7. Place short ribs on top of caramelized onion and garlic. Pour the beer on top of beef ribs.
8. Cover and place the pan in oven at 225° F. Let it bake for 2 hours.
9. Add BBQ sauce, cover, and cook for another 1 1/2 hours or until temperature inside the beef ribs reach 170° F.
10. Serve ribs over cheesy polenta or mashed potatoes.

BEER PAIRING: Contains Nuts Peanut Butter Milk Stout

Photos: Page 26, middle

Browncoat Risotto with Beef Short Rib

SUBMITTED BY: CARL SCHREIBER, FOM/HEAD CHEF—LTS BREWING CO., ROCHESTER

A unique take on a classic risotto dish, showcasing Browncoat, LTS Brewing Company's London Brown Ale. Subtle notes from the red wine and heat from the crushed pepper help to round the nutty, malty characters of the beer.

Short Ribs:

- 3-4 lbs short ribs
- 3 c Browncoat, London Brown Ale
- 1 c dry red wine, like Syrah
- 1 tbsp crushed red pepper
- 1 tsp cracked peppercorns
- salt, to taste

Risotto:

- 2 c arborio rice
- 4 c Browncoat, London Brown Ale
- 1 c beef stock
- 1 c vegetable stock
- 2 tbsp lemon juice
- 2 tbsp salted butter
- 2 medium shallots, minced
- 6 oz oyster or shitake mushrooms, diced

SERVES 4–6

For the Short Ribs:

1. Preheat oven to 300° F.
2. In a sauce pan over medium-low heat, add Browncoat; stir occasionally to prevent sticking. Once the beer has reduced by 1/3, remove from heat and stir in red wine. Return to medium heat until the edge of the liquid begins to bubble. Remove from heat and set aside.
3. In a small dish, combine the crushed red pepper, peppercorns, and salt. Rub each rib generously with spice blend.
4. Place ribs evenly in a roasting pan. Drizzle 1/2 the sauce over the ribs; cover. Roast on the middle rack of the oven for 1 hour, remove and spoon the pan sauce over the ribs several times (add remaining sauce if necessary). Cover and return to oven.
5. Repeat this process every 30 minutes until the ribs begin to fall apart, about 90 minutes. Remove from oven; rest. Transfer roasting liquid to sauce pan; reduce by 1/2. Set aside.

For the Risotto (begin after basting short ribs for the first time):

1. Add butter to a large sauté pan over medium heat. Add shallots to melted butter and cook until translucent.
2. Reduce heat to medium-low; add mushrooms; continue stirring for about 2–3 minutes. Add the rice and stir until the butter coats the rice evenly.
3. Add 1 cup of Browncoat, stirring constantly. When the rice has absorbed the beer, add the next cup. Repeat this process for the remaining beer and both stocks, stirring constantly. When all the liquid has been absorbed, remove from heat and stir in the lemon juice.
4. Plate the risotto and place a short rib directly in the center of the risotto. Finish with the reduced sauce.

BEER PAIRING: *Citrus-forward West Coast Style IPAs*

Honey Porter Braised Short Rib Cottage Pie

SUBMITTED BY: GREYSON ALTMOSE, TWIN CITIES CHEF, AND MATT ASAY, HEAD BREWER AND OWNER—FORGOTTEN STAR BREWING COMPANY, FRIDLEY

Greyson prepares this dish for his family on special occasions or when he's just craving something rich, decadent, and hearty. Forgotten Star Honey Porter is used in the braising process; it is a very robust beer that brings out the rich flavors of the beef short rib.

Short Ribs:

4 lb	bone-in short ribs, split into individual ribs
2	crowlers FSBC Boiler Room Honey Porter
2	carrots, unpeeled & chopped
1	large yellow onion, chopped
8	cloves garlic, crushed
1 qt	beef stock
2 tbsp	olive oil
2 tbsp	butter
	pepper & kosher salt

Gravy:

2	carrots, peeled & diced
1	large onion, diced
1 c	frozen peas
2 tbsp	butter
2 tbsp	olive oil
1/3 c	flour

Potatoes:

3 lbs	Yukon gold potatoes, peeled & diced
1 c	whole milk
8 tbsp	butter, cubed & chilled
3 c	shredded Kerrygold Irish Cheddar cheese
	pepper & kosher salt

SERVES 6–8

For the Short Ribs:

1. Trim fat from short ribs and season liberally with salt and pepper.
2. In a large stock pot, heat 2 tablespoons of olive oil over medium-high heat. Place ribs in the pot and brown on each side, about 2 minutes per side. Remove from pot and set aside.
3. Melt 2 tablespoons of butter in the same pot and add onions, carrots, and garlic. Cook until slightly tender, stirring occasionally, about 8 minutes.
4. Add one crowler of porter to deglaze; breaking up any brown bits in the bottom of the pan. Bring beer to a boil and reduce to a simmer for 5-8 minutes.
5. Add beef stock and return to boil then reduce to simmer, and place short ribs in the pot. Add second crowler of porter, cover pot and simmer on low for 3 hours until short ribs are tender.

For the Potatoes *(start cooking 2 hours into the braising process)*:

1. Place potatoes in large stock pot and cover with water. Bring covered pot to a boil over high heat. Once boiling, remove cover and simmer for 15 minutes until potatoes are tender.
2. Drain potatoes and place back in the pot with butter, milk, and 2 cups cheese. Mash together until creamy and smooth. Season with salt and pepper, set aside.

Assembly:

1. Once short ribs have finished, heat oven to 375° F.
2. Remove short ribs from pot, discard bones and fatty membrane. Shred ribs and set aside. Strain the solids and reserve the braising liquid for the gravy.
3. In the empty stock pot, melt 2 tablespoons butter with 2 tablespoons olive oil; sauté the carrots and onions until tender, about 5 minutes.

continued on pg. 29»»

4. Add the flour and stir until cooked and slightly toasted. Pour in the reserved braising liquid and stir to create the gravy. Simmer until thickened, about 15 minutes.
5. Once thickened, turn off heat and add shredded short ribs and peas. Fold all ingredients together until evenly combined.
6. Butter a 9"x13" casserole dish or eight 12–16 oz gratin dishes, and spoon short rib mixture evenly in the bottom of the dish/dishes. (If using individual dishes, fill about 1/2 full.)
7. Top with mashed potatoes, starting around the edges to create a seal to prevent mixture from bubbling up, and smooth with a spatula. (You can also use a piping bag with a large rosette tip, and pipe over top until completely covered.) Sprinkle remaining cheese over the top of the potatoes.
8. Place dish/dishes in the oven on a baking sheet baking for 15–20 minutes or until potatoes begin to brown. Remove from oven and let stand for 15 minutes. Serve and enjoy!

BEER PAIRING: *Big Stick IPA or other crisp, clean, and hoppy beers*

BAMF'D Tri-Tip

SUBMITTED BY: SHAUN LILL, HEAD BREWER & JORDAN GARCIA, ASSISTANT TO THE HEAD BREWER—HEADFLYER BREWING, MINNEAPOLIS

Shaun combined his passion for beer with his love of smoked meats and came up with this recipe that is perfect for a cool, autumn day. Using HeadFlyer's barrel-aged imperial stout, along with coffee from neighboring Five Watt Coffee, this recipe for smoked tri-tip is savory and sweet, with just a pinch of heat. Look for BAMF'D available annually in early November and grab a couple of bottles; one for cooking, and one for pairing. Cheers!

2 lb	tri-tip steak
1/4 c	Five Watt Dark Roast ground coffee
1/4 c	brown sugar
1 tsp	ground cinnamon
1 tsp	cayenne
1 tbsp	coarse salt
1 tbsp	coarse black pepper
1/2 c	HeadFlyer Brewing BAMF'D
1/4 c	HeadFlyer Brewing BAMF'D for glaze (optional)

Special Equipment:
- Smoker

SERVES 4–6

1. Two hours before smoking, place tri-tip on the counter to come to room temperature.
2. Combine seasonings, coffee, and beer in a small bowl, and whisk together until well mixed, to use as a marinade. Pour marinade into a gallon zip-seal bag, and add the tri-tip. Seal bag, removing as much air as possible. Rub bag around the tri-tip, completely covering it in the marinade. Let sit on counter for 1 hour.
3. Heat smoker to 225° F, using a hickory blend of pellets or chips.
4. Remove tri-tip from marinade, and discard the marinade. Place tri-tip in the center of the smoker grate, insert temperature probe.
5. Smoke until the temperature probe reads 135° F, and remove.
6. Wrap the tri-tip in foil, and place back in smoker for 15 minutes, OR heat a cast iron skillet to high, add 1/4 cup Headflyer Brewing BAMF'D and tri-tip into the skillet, and cook 2 minutes per side to get a nice sweet crispy glaze.
7. Move tri-tip to a cutting board, and let it rest for 15 minutes. For best results, cut and serve with a goblet of HeadFlyer BAMF'D.

BEER PAIRING: HeadFlyer Brewing BAMF'D, HeadFlyer Brewing Vanilla Bean Porter, Stout, or Lager

Photos: Page 32, top left & right

Town Hall Shepherds Pie

SUBMITTED BY: MIKE HANSON, CORPORATE CHEF, AND MIKE HOOPS, HEAD BREWER—
TOWN HALL BREWERY, MINNEAPOLIS

Town Hall Brewery's version of a brewpub classic. Lamb, onions, garlic, peas, and potatoes. They added one of their Town Hall signature beers, H2O Oatmeal Stout, as well as some Dubliner cheddar cheese to give this dish some great flavors.

Potatoes:

3 lbs	potatoes, peeled & quartered
2 c	heavy cream
2	egg yolks
1 lb	Dubliner cheddar cheese, shredded
1 tbsp	kosher salt
1 tbsp	ground black pepper

Filling:

2 tbsp	oil
1 lb	white onion, diced
3 lbs	ground lamb or beef
3/4 lb	carrots, peeled & diced
2 oz	garlic, chopped
1/2 c	flour
2 tbsp	dried rosemary
2 tbsp	dired thyme
2 tsp	kosher salt
2 tsp	ground black pepper
1 c	peas or English peas
1 c	corn
1/4 c	Worcestershire
2 c	Town Hall H2O Oatmeal Stout

SERVES 4–6

1. Preheat oven to 350° F.
2. Peel and quarter potatoes and place in a soup pot. Cover with water and bring to a boil. Cook for 15–20 minutes, or until potatoes can be pierced easily with a fork. Drain water and set aside.
3. In a new pot, heat oil and cook onions until translucent. Add ground lamb or beef and the carrots. Cook until meat is browned. Add garlic.
4. Mix in flour and cook for an additional 2–3 minutes to create a roux.
5. Add the remaining filling ingredients. Cook for another couple minutes until liquid thickens. Turn off heat and allow to rest while you finish the potatoes.
6. Add heavy cream to the potatoes and mix with a whisk or mixer. Add in cheese, egg yolks, salt and pepper.
7. Divide your lamb into two pans. Carefully spread the potatoes over the top, making sure you create a seal around the pan so the liquid does not boil over.
8. Place pans in the preheated oven and bake for about 20 minutes. Potatoes will be caramelized on top when finished. Garnish with a little chopped parsley.

BEER PAIRING: Hope and King Scotch Ale, or darker beers such as a stout, and bourbon barrel-aged beers

Photo: Page 32, middle

Chocolate Stout Cake

SUBMITTED BY: MELISSA LEDDY, CO-OWNER, AND LANGSETH FAMILY—
BACK CHANNEL BREWING, SPRING PARK

Melissa and family bake this Chocolate Stout Cake annually on St. Patty's Day.

Cake:

1 c	Back Channel stout
1 c	unsalted butter (2 sticks) + 1 tbsp
2 c	sugar
2 c	all-purpose flour
3/4 c	cocoa powder
2/3 c	sour cream
2	eggs
1 tbsp	vanilla
2 1/2 tsp	baking soda

Frosting:

1	8 oz package cream cheese (room temp)
1 1/4 c	powdered sugar
2 tsp	cornstarch
1/2 c	heavy cream

SERVES 8–12

1. Preheat oven to 350° F.
2. Butter & line a 9" springform tin.
3. Pour stout into a large saucepan, add butter (cut into cubes) and heat until melted. Whisk in cocoa and sugar.
4. In separate bowl, beat the sour cream with eggs and vanilla, then pour into pan with mixture.
5. Whisk in the flour and baking soda.
6. Pour the batter into a greased and lined tin, and bake for 45 minutes to 1 hour.
7. Cool (in tin) on a cooling rack—cake should be damp. Once cool, sit it on a flat surface to frost.
8. For Frosting: Whip the cream cheese in mixing bowl until smooth. Sift the powdered sugar and cornstarch and then beat to combine. Add heavy cream and beat frosting until it's a spreadable consistency.
9. Frost the top of cake–think foam on a dark roasty stout.

BEER PAIRING: Smitty Cakes Imperial Stout or any Back Channel Brewing Stout

Photo: Page 32, bottom

Peanut Butter Apple Crumble

SUBMITTED BY: RICK DIDORA, WIZARD OF CULINARY ENDEAVORS—
DANGEROUS MAN BREWING CO, MINNEAPOLIS

Dangerous Man Brewing Company infused this spin on an apple crumble with their Peanut Butter Porter to bring in a roasty nuttiness to this autumnal classic.

4 c	apples, chopped to 1" cubes
1 c	Peanut Butter Porter
1/4 c	sugar
1 tbsp	cornstarch
1/2 tsp	cinnamon
2/3 c	brown sugar, packed
3/4 c	flour
6 tbsp	butter
1 tbsp	lemon juice
pinch	salt

SERVES 6–8

1. Preheat oven to 375° F.
2. Butter an 8x8 inch baking dish.
3. Combine apples with PB Porter in medium bowl. Stir to cover as needed. Let stand 15–20 minutes while preparing other ingredients.
4. Add sugar, cornstarch and cinnamon in small bowl and mix to combine.
5. Using fingers, mix together brown sugar, flour, butter and salt into a coarse, gravel-like crumble.
6. Drain off 1/2 cup of PB Porter from apples, then add sugar cornstarch mixture and lemon juice. Toss to coat.
7. Add apples to baking dish; top with crumble.
8. Bake for 45–50 minutes or until top is crispy golden brown.

BEER PAIRING: Dangerous Man Peanut Butter Porter

Photos: Page 36, top left & right

Dangerous Man Brewing Co. is a destination microbrewery & taproom in NE Minneapolis, operating since 2013. Their focus is high-quality, small-batch production beers with ever-changing taps.

Lift Bridge Stout Brownies

SUBMITTED BY: BRAD GLYNN, CO-OWNER AND VP OF MARKETING—
LIFT BRIDGE BREWERY, STILLWATER

Brad developed this stout brownie recipe to put right on the grill after dinner. This mouthwatering recipe is great with your favorite local stouts.

1/2 c	butter + 2 tbsp
1 c	Lift Bridge Irish Coffee Stout or Silhouette Imperial Stout–reduced from 12 oz
1 c	semi-sweet chocolate chips
2	large eggs
1/2 c	sugar + 1 tbsp
1 tsp	vanilla extract
1/3 c	flour
1 tsp	baking powder
1/4 tsp	salt

SERVES 8–12

1. Before starting on brownies, reduce 1 1/2 cups of Lift Bridge Irish Coffee Stout or Silhouette Imperial Stout to 1 cup.
2. In a microwave on medium heat or using a double boiler, melt 1/2 cup chocolate chips with 1 stick of butter until melted and set aside to cool.
3. In a separate bowl, add eggs, 1/2 cup beer reduction, sugar, and vanilla and stir. Add chocolate mixture to the egg mixture and stir to incorporate. Add flour, baking powder, and salt to the liquid mixture and stir to incorporate.
4. Pour into buttered cast iron pan (one 10" or two 4 1/2") and place on the grill over low coals or indirect (350° F) heat for 30 minutes. Check with a toothpick.
5. Take remaining 1/2 cup chocolate chips, 2 tablespoons butter, 1 tablespoon sugar, and 1/2 cup stout beer reduction and melt over low heat in microwave or double boiler until smooth. Allow to cool and pour over brownies just before serving.

BEER PAIRING: Irish Coffee Stout or Warden Milk Stout, or any stout

Photo: Page 36, middle

Stoneware Stout Chocolate Cake

SUBMITTED BY: RED WING BREWERY, RED WING

For over a century, Red Wing has been known for its quality stoneware. Now, it's also known for its indulgent Stoneware Stout Chocolate Cake! Incredibly moist and glazed with a rich ganache, this is the perfect treat for chocolate lovers.

Cake:

- 2 c all-purpose flour
- 2 c sugar
- 1/4 c brown sugar
- 1/2 c unsweetened cocoa powder
- 1 tsp salt
- 2 tsp baking soda
- 3/4 c vegetable oil
- 4 tsp white vinegar
- 1 tsp vanilla extract
- 1 tsp almond extract
- 1 1/2 c Stoneware Stout
- 1/2 c water

Ganache:

- 1 c heavy whipping cream
- 1/2 c semi-sweet chocolate
- 1/2 c milk chocolate
- 1 tbsp instant coffee

SERVES 12

1. Preheat oven to 350° F.
2. In a large bowl, combine dry ingredients together and sift. Make one large well and two small wells in the mixture.
3. Pour vegetable oil in the large well, vinegar in one of the small wells, and vanilla and almond extracts in the other small well. Pour Stoneware Stout over the entire mixture, then add water. Mix thoroughly.
4. Pour into a greased 9"x13" pan and bake for around 40 minutes or until a toothpick inserted in the center comes out clean.
5. Near the end of the bake, combine ganache ingredients in a medium saucepan and stir constantly over medium heat until the chocolate has melted and the mixture is smooth.
6. Pour over entire pan of cake or drizzle over individual pieces. If ganache becomes too firm, slightly reheat to desired consistency.

BEER PAIRING: Stoneware Stout or any dark & roasty beer

Photo: Page 36, bottom

The first brewery in the city since 1951, Red Wing Brewery opened their doors in 2012 and features historical beers from Red Wing's past, today's favorites, and root beer.

Fruity, Spicy, Tart & Funky

Beers with a fruity, spicy, tart, or funky flavor profile can be found in every beer style, but you'll most likely find these flavors in sours, kettle sours, Berliner Weissbiers, IPAs, and lambics.

When snacking along with an FSTF beer, root vegetables, rich meats, and earthy cheeses can help highlight the unique beer flavors. Tart beers can also act as a good palate cleanser when eating spicy and fatty foods.

Cooking with FSTF beers is always an experiment in flavor! Cooking with a bright and salty gose will give you an entirely different experience than the same recipe with a cherry lambic. When you're working with the following recipes, start off with a beer similar to what is recommended.

Kieran's Rhubarb Gold Cuban Sandwich 39
FINNEGANS

Wild Mushroom Pasta 41
August Schell Brewing Company

Kriek Braised and Glazed Beef Short Ribs 42
Pig Ate My Pizza Kitchen & Brewery

Popper Ribs 44
Wabasha Brewing Co.

Kieran's Rhubarb Gold Cuban Sandwich

SUBMITTED BY: CHEF AARON UBAN, CULINARY MANAGER FOR KIERAN'S KITCHEN WITH FINNEGANS, MINNEAPOLIS

Thinking about a potential joint menu item with FINNEGANS, Chef Aaron made his way down to the brewery and sampled many of their current offerings. This is when he discovered FINNEGANS Rhubarb Gold, a big brett beer aged in oak barrels on 260 pounds of local rhubarb. He remembers the overall boldness, balance, and complexity of the beer immediately railroading any preconceived notions of potential food pairings.

He was immediately struck with the mental image of a huge, melty squished pork sandwich getting eaten while ice fishing and listening to some Cuban Bolero music. He could taste the pickles, the salinity of the cheese. The crust of expertly smashed Filone baguette, cumin, mustard...this is how this sandwich happened.

Pulled Pork:

- 1 pork shoulder
- 2 tbsp salt
- vegetable oil
- 2 sweet yellow onions, finely diced
- 6 parsnips, peeled & finely diced
- 3/4 celery root, peeled & finely diced
- 2 tbsp Aleppo or chili powder
- 1 tbsp cumin
- 2 tbsp tamarind paste
- 64 oz pork or chicken stock
- 3 sprigs fresh thyme
- 3 cloves garlic, crushed
- 2 bay leaves, whole
- 64 oz Rhubarb Gold beer (1 growler)

SERVES 2–4

For the Pork:

1. Cut the pork shoulder in pieces small enough to assemble into a large, wide pot and coat liberally with salt. In a very hot pot, pour a little vegetable oil and immediately sear the pork shoulder. Turn it often to keep from scorching, but allow a fair amount of color to develop. Remove pork and rest on a sheet pan.
2. Add more oil to the pot and, using high heat, add your onions and garlic. Sauté until soft, then add parsnip and celery root along with your Aleppo/chili powder and cumin. Stir this around and allow it to toast. Add the tamarind. Stir and put the pork back in and stir again.
3. Add all remaining ingredients and bring to a simmer over medium-high heat. Cover and reduce heat; simmer very slowly for 4+ hours. The meat is ready when it can be pulled apart with tongs. Cool overnight in its braising liquid. Put on the lowest available shelf in the refrigerator.

Preparing Pulled Pork

1. Separate the pork from the braise liquid and vegetables. Discard your bay leaves (there were 2), thyme sprigs, and the layer of pork fat that has risen to the top and solidified.
2. Reheat the braise liquid and vegetables. Use an immersion blender to buzz up the vegetables to create a nice thick sauce.
3. Reintroduce your pork and reheat to a minimum of 165° F, stirring it around often, and start the process of pulling it apart. Add salt as needed.

continued on pg.40 »»

Sandwich Fixings:

1/4 lb	pulled pork
1	Bakersfield Filone baguette (or other baguette)
1/2 tbsp	Dijon mustard
1/2 tbsp	mayo
6-8	pickles of choice
2-3	thick slices Alemar Good Thunder cheese (or other funky soft cheese)
1/8 lb	thinly sliced ham

Preparing the Sandwiches:

1. Have your pulled pork hot, turn on your sandwich press, or heat skillet.
2. Slice a baguette lengthwise almost all of the way through. Open it up like a butterfly and place the cut side down on the skillet to toast. At the same time, place ham on the skillet to sear.
3. Remove your bread and smear mustard on one side and mayo on the other and place your pickles. Flip your ham over to sear other side.
4. Place the freshly seared ham on top of the pickles. Add a nice helping of pulled pork on top of the ham. Top with cheese.
5. Close the sandwich and place on the skillet. Either close the top of your panini press, or utilize a balancing act of cookie sheet and weights to smash the sandwich down. Juices will make splattering noises, the cheese will wake up and become fragrant, the bits that fall out of the baguette will start to caramelize, but you must be patient. Allow enough time to properly warm the bread through.
6. When ready, transport the Cuban to a cutting board, carefully slice it in half, and place it on a plate.
7. Now sit down on your folding chair, careful not to knock over your tackle box. Take a second to have a nice big sip of your glass of Rhubarb Gold. Feel that tartness hit your pucker button. Now check your fish lines, you don't want to lose out on a monster walleye just because you are eating a sandwich. You need to make sure everything is good. Have a nice big bite. Have a nice big sip. Sit back, close your eyes and know that yes, "everything is good."

BEER PAIRING: FINNEGANS Rhubarb Gold

Wild Mushroom Pasta

SUBMITTED BY: JACE MARTI, ASSISTANT BREWMASTER—
AUGUST SCHELL BREWING COMPANY, NEW ULM

This is a recipe that Jace loves to make with fresh-picked, wild mushrooms, but it can also be made with store-bought varieties. The sour beer reduction adds a ton of flavor to the mushrooms and helps to make a creamy, decadent sauce. This is a rich, luxurious recipe that comes together quickly and can be enjoyed any night of the week.

1 lb	mushrooms (chanterelles or porcini, and/or store bought varieties like cremini, oyster or shiitake)
1 lb	fettuccine noodles
2	medium shallots or 1 small yellow onion, finely chopped
4	medium cloves garlic, finely chopped
1/4 c	olive oil
2 tbsp	butter
1	lemon
1/2 c	heavy whipping cream
1/4 c	mixed-culture golden sour beer
	salt & pepper to taste
	fresh-grated Parmesan
	fresh parsley

SERVES 4

1. Clean mushrooms using a damp cloth or brush (do not rinse with water as the mushrooms will absorb the water) and break into quarters or thick slices, depending on the type of mushroom you are using.
2. Bring a pot of salted water to a boil, cook pasta as directed, but 1-2 minutes short of al dente.
3. Drain, reserving at least 1 cup of pasta water.
4. Preheat a large skillet over medium-high heat, add the olive oil and heat until shimmering.
5. Add the mushrooms to skillet, stir to coat, and then sear, undisturbed about 5 minutes.
6. When the mushrooms develop a golden-brown color, stir and allow sear again several more minutes.
7. When the mushrooms are evenly browned, add 2 tablespoons of butter, garlic, and shallots. Cook 1–2 minutes, stirring frequently, or until the shallots and garlic are golden and fragrant.
8. Season with salt and pepper, then add 1/4 cup of sour beer and reduce the mixture over medium heat. When the beer has reduced, add the heavy cream and reduce again, about 2 minutes. Squeeze with lemon juice, and season with salt and pepper if needed.
9. Add the cooked pasta to the mixture, with about 1 cup of pasta water. Stir thoroughly to coat, and continue to cook until pasta water is absorbed and sauce has thickened slightly.
10. Remove from heat and allow pasta to stand for a few minutes. Sauce will thicken as it cools.
11. Serve garnished with Parmesan and parsley to taste.

BEER PAIRING: Static Transmission, or any mixed culture golden sour

Photo: Page 43, top left

Kriek Braised and Glazed Beef Short Ribs
with Rice Lager Jasmine Rice

SUBMITTED BY: ANDY GOETTSCH, HEAD BREWER, AND NATHANIEL MOSER, CHEF DE CUISINE—
PIG ATE MY PIZZA KITCHEN AND BREWERY, ROBBINSDALE

Andy makes these rich and sweet short ribs at home with his family. They're super easy to make and great for any occasion. Cooking the ribs sous vide ensures the perfect cook without having to baby sit, so you can drink that other bottle of kriek you bought. If you're able, cold smoke the ribs before marinating for extra flavor!

SERVES 4–6

Marinade:
- 1/2 yellow onion
- 4 cloves garlic
- 2 oz fresh ginger, peeled
- 1 c soy sauce
- 1 c brown sugar
- 1/4 c mirin
- 1 tbsp sesame oil
- pinch chili flakes
- 750 mL cherry lambic or kriek
- 4 bone slab beef short ribs
- salt and pepper

Rice:
- 1 c jasmine rice
- 12 oz rice lager
- 1 tbsp mirin

Garnish:
- sliced green onion
- toasted sesame seeds
- fresh cilantro

1. Place onion, garlic, ginger, soy, sugar, mirin, sesame, and chili flakes in a blender and blend on high until smooth. Blend in the kriek (watch out for foaming).
2. Cut the short ribs into individual bones and season with salt and pepper.
3. Seal the ribs and half the marinade (the other half will be used for glaze) in a vacuum seal bag (or gallon ziplock). Marinate ribs in the bag in the fridge for 12–18 hours.
4. After marination, set up an immersion circulator at 185° F and cook the ribs in the same bag for 10–12 hours. (Alternate Method: Place marinade and beef in Dutch oven and heat on stove top until simmering, cover and cook in oven at 185° F for 10–12 hours).
5. Meanwhile, slowly reduce the other half of the marinade by 1/2, or until the consistency reaches that of a thick pastry stout. Set aside in the fridge.
6. After the ribs have finished cooking, remove from bag (or Dutch oven), discard the cooking liquid, and place ribs on a baking sheet covered in tin foil, meat side up. Brush or spoon the glaze over the ribs and place into a 425° F oven for 10 minutes total, basting 3–4 more times, until the glaze forms a tacky crust. A little burnt sugar is OK here, it is the good stuff!
7. Rinse the rice in a colander 5 times or until the water runs clear. Place in a pot with lager and mirin and bring to a boil. Turn down to a simmer, cover, and cook for 10 minutes. Turn off heat; rest covered for 5 minutes.
8. Top rice with a beautifully glazed short rib, hit it with more glaze if you have it and sprinkle with toasted sesame seeds, sliced green onion and picked cilantro.

BEER PAIRING: Lambics or other tart or sour beers, pale ales, pilsners

Photo: Page 43, bottom

Popper Ribs

SUBMITTED BY: BRETT ERICKSON, HEAD BREWER—WABASHA BREWING CO., ST. PAUL

Brett was a Competition BBQ chef from 2009–2015. The rub on these ribs is what he used in competition and the sauce is a store-bought sauce with a super-simple addition to just take it up a notch.

Rub:

1	rack of ribs
1/2 c	brown sugar
2 tsp	smoked paprika
1 tbsp	coarse salt
2 tbsp	black pepper
1 tsp	cayenne pepper
1/2 tsp	garlic pepper
1/2 tsp	onion pepper

Sauce:

3 1/2 oz	spicy BBQ sauce (such as Wee Willie's)
2 oz	Wabasha Brewing Co. West Side Popper

Rib Baste:

1/2 c	brown sugar
3/4 c	Wabasha Brewing Co. West Side Popper

Special Equipment:
- Smoker or grill

SERVES 2–4

1. Bring smoker to 250–275° F using applewood. Take ribs out of the refrigerator and let them come to room temperature.

2. Mix all dry-rub ingredients in a bowl or mason jar. Apply rub to ribs top and bottom...don't be shy, cover the ribs well and use the whole rub mixture.

3. Put ribs on smoker/grill and cover for 3 hours, maintaining the temperature of 250–275° F.

4. While cooking, take 3 1/2 ounces of spicy BBQ sauce and add Wabasha West Side Popper to thin out the sauce and make more of a glaze. Mix thoroughly.

5. At the 3-hour mark, pull the ribs from the smoker and set them on aluminum foil. Spread 1/2 cup of brown sugar on top of the ribs. Wrap the ribs in the foil, but before closing the foil, pour 3/4 cup of Wabasha West Side Popper into the foil pouch. Close foil pouch carefully so you don't accidentally puncture the foil pack. Heavy duty foil, or multiple layers of standard foil, works best.

6. Put the ribs in their foil pack back on grill for another 2 hours.

7. At the 2-hour mark, take ribs off grill and unwrap them. Carefully pick up ribs with tongs and put them back on the smoker/grill.

8. Mop the ribs with the BBQ sauce mixture. Close the smoker lid for 5 minutes to finish. Pull the ribs from the smoker and let them rest for 10–15 minutes. Cut and serve.

BEER PAIRING: Red Desert IPA

Photo: Page 43, top right

Hoppy & Bitter

If you love India Pale Ales and other Hoppy & Bitter craft beer, this is the chapter for you! Beers that fall into this category are heavy on their star ingredient, hops, but are often well-balanced with malts. There are an endless number of ways to describe the flavors in hop-heavy beers: floral, earthy, citrusy, piney, fruity, and bitter.

Hoppy & Bitter beers are perfect to drink alongside classic bar foods like chicken wings or pizza. The fat cuts the bitterness of your beer, while roasted flavors can help accentuate the maltiness.

Though cooking with an IPA or pale ale may seem complicated, we've brought in some experts to show you the way.

In this chapter, you'll find recipes for classic bar fare along with some surprisingly classy options. Try these recipes out with different beers to experience what hops can bring out in your meals.

Spiral Into This Cheese Dip 46
Spiral Brewery

Hot Dog Roller Level-Up 47
Modist Brewing

Excelsior BrewGrub Salmon Cake Sliders................................49
Excelsior Brewing Company

Dark Lager Beef Stacker 50
Imminent Brewing

Spiral Into This Cheese Dip

SUBMITTED BY: CHEF EMILY FROM THE ONION GRILLE WITH SPIRAL BREWERY, HASTINGS

Chef Emily's Beer Cheese Dip recipe from the Onion Grille in Hastings, MN is always a hit at Spiral Brewery. Created with Spiral's Downward Spiral IPA, the dip is tangy, cheesy, and delicious. Serve with a pub pretzel or your favorite cheese vessel.

1 c	butter
1 c	flour
2 tbsp	garlic, minced
4 c	heavy cream
4 c	water
1 tbsp	chicken base
1/2 c	mild cheddar
1/2 c	Gouda
1 1/2 c	Downward Spiral IPA

SERVES 10

1. Melt butter and add flour.
2. Add cream, water, garlic, chicken base, and cheese.
3. In a separate pan or pot, simmer beer for 3 minutes to cook alcohol off.
4. When cheese sauce thickens, incorporate beer. Enjoy!

BEER PAIRING: Spiral Brewery's Downward Spiral IPA

Photo: Page 48, top

Spiral Brewery opened in 2018 in Hastings, MN with a mission to brew community with quality beer and rich history. Enjoy one of their many beers on their rooftop patio or in their taproom.

Hot Dog Roller Level-Up *The Ultimate in Snack Carnage*

SUBMITTED BY: THE MISFIT CREW AT MODIST BREWING COMPANY, MINNEAPOLIS

It's not just beer that is being modified by the crew at Modist Brewing Company! The initially-controversial employee hot dog roller has served as another in a long line of things that have entered the building and been challenged beyond their conventional use. The staff at Modist is happy to share that hot dog roller machines aren't just for hot dogs!

1 package jalepeño poppers

1 package mozzarella sticks

1 package taquitos

Special Equipment:
- Hot Dog Roller Machine

SERVES 2–4

1. Set hot dog roller to 225° F.
2. Add mozzarella sticks, jalapeño poppers, and taquitos to the rollers. Flip and rotate items that aren't rolling on their own (some roll great, others need a little more help).
3. Once they're good and cooked to recommended temperature, dunk them in delectable sauce action.
4. When replenishing rollers, it is best to establish a system for replenishment understood by all who may be adding more snack carnage to the hot dog roller machine [Modist Brewing suggests following FOFO (first on first off)]. Most importantly, remember to clean it thoroughly (using a damp rag while it's still warm) so that next time you're ready to go full send on the snack train, you can enjoy without hesitation or worry that you may have lost power cord privileges for 2 weeks since it wasn't appropriately cleaned last time it was used.

BEER PAIRING: Dreamyard New England IPA

Photo: Page 48, bottom

Excelsior BrewGrub Salmon Cake Sliders

SUBMITTED BY: JOHN KLICK, FOUNDER BREWGRUB TRUCK, JOHN MIHAJLOV, FOUNDER, RESTAURANT INSPIRATION—EXCELSIOR BREWING COMPANY, EXCELSIOR

The BrewGrub truck at Excelsior Brewing Company was well-known for this delicious dish.

For Poaching Liquid:

3	bottles Dragon Fruit Milkshake IPA
1 tbsp	dill
2 tbsp	lime juice
1 tbsp	fish seasoning

For Salmon Cakes:

1 lb	salmon
2	egg yolks
1/8 c	mayonnaise
1/8 c	green onion, diced
1 tbsp	dill
1/2 tbsp	fish seasoning
1/2 tbsp	lime juice
1/2 tbsp	Worcestershire
1/2 tbsp	Dijon mustard
1 1/2 c	bread crumbs
dash	Tobasco
1/4 tsp	salt

For Sandwich:

- sandwich bread/buns
- sandwich fixings

MAKES 10–14 CAKES

1. In saucepan, heat Dragon Fruit Milkshake IPA to 212° F. Add dill, lime juice, and fish seasoning (Old Bay) to simmering liquid. Wait 5 minutes.
2. Add salmon and cook to medium (about 15 minutes). It is important the poaching liquid not boil and fish is completely covered.
3. Remove salmon and cool completely.
4. In a large bowl mix all ingredients except salmon and bread crumbs. Combine thoroughly.
5. Once cool, flake salmon into the mixture, folding in slowly to keep healthy chunks of salmon. Finally add bread crumbs (Panko works best) folding again to keep chunks of salmon. Cover mixture and let sit 2 hours.
6. After two hours, shape your patties. Each one should be 3 1/2 to 4 1/2 ounces.
7. Coat a fry pan with cooking oil, bring up to medium heat. Dredge patties in remaining bread crumbs and sauté until golden brown.
8. Add bun and fixings of your choice like tomato, avocado and roasted red pepper aioli.

BEER PAIRING: Dragon Fruit Milkshake IPA

Photo: Page 52, top

Dark Lager Beef Stacker

SUBMITTED BY: IMMINENT BREWING WITH GWEN ANDERSON, OWNER & OPERATOR OF THE LOCAL PLATE—NORTHFIELD

This recipe, a collaboration between Imminent Brewing and The Local Plate, evolved from two experiences: a beer pairing pop-up dinner, and 2018 MNCBG Winterfest. At the dinner, Gwen tried out a recipe for 'Carbonnade a la Flamande' (Flemish Beef Stew) and at Winterfest, The Local Plate paired with Imminent Brewing to offer skewers of a stacked sourdough bread/brie/Gouda/roasted tomato/caramelized onion! This recipe is a combination of both—an amped-up, double-decker grilled stacker of a sammie. As members of the Cannon Valley Grown marketing collaborative, Imminent Brewing always uses products from farmers and producers in the Cannon River watershed region: tomatoes from Waxwing Farm, cheese from Cannon Belles Cheese, onions from Seeds Farm, beef from HD Beef Works, and bread from Brick Oven Bakery.

3	pints cherry tomatoes
2 tsp	olive oil
3	large yellow onions
1 lb	butter
1/2 lb	Gouda cheese
1/4 lb	bacon, diced
2 lb	beef stew meat (or any type of roast works well; cut into 1" chunks)
2 c	Imminent Clever Dark Lager (or other medium-bodied dark/malty beer)
1 tbsp	tomato paste
2	bay leaves
	salt & pepper
12-18	slices of sourdough or white bakery bread

SERVES 4–6

1. Roasted Cherry Tomatoes: Toss the cherry tomatoes with the olive oil and 1 teaspoon salt. Spread on a baking sheet and roast at 325° F for about 1 hour until collapsed and juicy. Refrigerate until ready to use.
2. Caramelized Onions: Slice 3 large yellow onions into 1/4" slivers. Melt one stick butter in a sauce pan. Add onions and cook over medium-low heat, stirring frequently, until well-browned. Refrigerate until ready to use.
3. Shred Gouda cheese with large grater or with a food processor, refrigerate (covered) until ready to use.

For the Braised Beef and Bacon:

1. Preheat oven to 325° F.
2. In a Dutch oven (or other oven-proof cooking vessel) over medium heat on the stove, sauté bacon until fat is rendered and bacon is starting to brown. Add the beef chunks, and sauté until no longer pink. Salt and pepper to taste.
3. Pour the beer over the beef; stir in the tomato paste and throw in the bay leaves. Bring the mixture to a simmer.
4. Cover the pan (with a lid or tight-fitting aluminum foil) and put in the oven. Braise for about 2 hours—the beef should fall apart.
5. Remove beef chunks and the bacon from pan with slotted spoon (save the remaining juices if you'd like to create a gravy) and refrigerate until ready to use.

continued on pg.51 »»

For the Stackers:

1. Butter two of the slices of bread on one side each (for the OUTSIDE of the stack).
2. Put the sammie together by layering one slice (buttered side DOWN) and loading it with a layer each of roasted tomatoes, the beef, shredded Gouda and caramelized onion.
3. Top that layer with a third, unbuttered slice of bread, and then load it up with the same sequence of ingredients as above.
4. Close up the stacker with the other slice of buttered bread, buttered side OUT. Repeat for additional stackers.
5. Heat a flat pan or griddle to medium and add 1 tablespoon butter per sammie you're going to cook at one time. Place the stacker(s) in the pan, and squish down well with a big spatula!
6. Cook until golden brown, then carefully flip over and cook the other side. The cheese should be nice and melted. Tip: If you're making multiple batches you can hold the stacker warm in a 175° F oven on a baking sheet until they're all done.
7. Cut in half on a cutting board, plate, and enjoy with your favorite beer!

BEER PAIRING: Dragon Squirrel Juicy IPA, or your favorite pale ale or IPA

Photo: Page 52, bottom

Imminent Brewing, est. June 2017, is a small production brewery and taproom in downtown Northfield, MN. Their mission is to create space for community: kind humans (of all ages) are invited to gather in the taproom (or on the patio!) to find good conversations over a fresh, local brew. Their motto is "it's about time," meant to convey their dedication to taking time to carefully craft their beers (using local ingredients wherever possible!), as well as their deep belief in spending quality time with friends and neighbors supporting local music, food trucks, small business folks, farms, and community.

Malty & Sweet

The Malty & Sweet category includes milk stouts, brown ales, Oktoberfests, amber ales, porters, and more. These beers have subtle, warm, and mildly sweet flavors. It is an excellent category for those who are just starting to explore craft beer.

When enjoying these beers alongside food, you can pair them with braised meats or other smoky flavors to help elevate the malts. They are also delicious with roasted veggies and many desserts! This category is one of the most versatile, so it's no wonder it has the most recipes!

Beer-Battered Shrimp.................54
Barley John's Brewpub

Campfire 14° ESB Philly Cheesesteak 55
Bent Paddle Brewing Company

Ursa Minor Brewing Pizza Dough 57
Ursa Minor Brewing

Brewhall Pizza............................58
Shakopee Brewhall

Mussels de Belgique....................59
Blacklist Brewing Co.

Amber Pot Pie 61
Waconia Brewing Company

Truth Be Told Pork Belly...............63
Angry Inch Brewing

Coq au Bier................................64
The Freehouse

Trails Giving Turkey 66
Copper Trail Brewing

Wee Heavy Creme Brulee 67
10K Brewing

Sticky Toffee Pudding.................68
Little Thistle Brewing Co.

Peanut Butter Stout Pudding.......70
Revelation Ale Works

Vanilla Latte Caramel Cream 71
Urban Growler

Beer-Battered Shrimp *with Beer Reduction*

SUBMITTED BY: JOHN MOORE, BREWMASTER/OWNER, AND TYLER WAHL, COOK—BARLEY JOHN'S BREWPUB, NEW BRIGHTON

Beer-battered seafood is a long-standing Minnesota tradition. Taking it a step further, this is a beer-battered shrimp paired with a sticky, sweet, spicy, and ever-so-slightly bitter beer reduction with an Asian flair. This take on fried shrimp is perfect for cocktail parties, especially on a cool fall evening.

SERVES 2–6

Sauce:

1 c	Wild Brunette beer
1 c	dark brown sugar, packed
1 tbsp	ginger, freshly grated
2 tbsp	garlic, chopped
1 tbsp	crushed red pepper
1 tbsp	salt
1 tsp	cinnamon
zest	of 1 orange
1/4 c	orange juice
1/4 c	lime juice
1/8 c	cornstarch slurry

Dredge:

1/2 c	high-gluten flour
1 tbsp	cornstarch
1 tsp	salt

Batter:

2/3 c	high-gluten flour
1/3 c	rice flour
1 tbsp	cornstarch
1 tbsp	garlic powder
2 tbsp	salt
1 tsp	black pepper
1/2 tbsp	ginger powder
1	egg
1 1/2 c	Wild Brunette beer
	raw shrimp, thawed & butterflied

1. Grate ginger, chop garlic.
2. Combine all sauce ingredients in a sauce pot and bring to a slow simmer. Reduce by half.
3. Prepare dredge by mixing flours, cornstarch and salt.
4. Prepare batter by mixing all dry ingredients and the egg with a whisk. Once mixed together, add beer gradually (half a cup at a time whilst whisking) to obtain a consistency slightly thicker than that of water.
5. Once the beer reduction has reduced to half volume, add the slurry and whisk to thicken over low heat. Cool slightly before serving.
6. Toss shrimp in dredge, making sure to completely coat. Take dredged shrimp and entirely coat in beer batter.
7. Lower gently into 350° F frying oil, cook approximately 3 minutes until golden brown.
8. Drain shrimp onto paper towel and lightly season with salt and black pepper. Serve on a bed of greens with the sauce on the side to dip or drizzled over for an easy passed appetizer.

BEER PAIRING: Wild Brunette Wild Rice Ale

Photo: Page 56, top left & right

Campfire 14° ESB Philly Cheesesteak

SUBMITTED BY: MAXWELL MCGRUDER, PROFESSIONAL BEER DRINKER—
BENT PADDLE BREWING COMPANY, DULUTH

The Campfire 14° ESB Philly Cheesesteak is a great recipe for anyone who is a fan of "Car Camping" or cooking over a fire in general. Pack your meats, prep your veggies, and get ready for one of the easiest, tastiest recipes sure to please the whole crew. The combined sweetness of the peppers, rolls, and malt complement the bittersweetness brought out by the onion & hops, flavors which are encapsulated in every bite of steak. Enjoy!

1 1/2 lb	thin cut flank or stir fry beef
1	red pepper
1	green pepper
1	white onion
4 tbsp	garlic
2 tbsp	extra virgin olive oil
2 tsp	Italian seasoning
18 oz	Bent Paddle 14° ESB
2	12-count packs Hawaiian sweet rolls
1 lb	provolone cheese, sliced

Special Equipment:
- Cast Iron Dutch Oven
- Fire Pit

MAKES 12

1. Get bed of coals going in fire pit.
2. Julienne the red and green pepper and white onion.
3. Combine beef, peppers and onions, garlic, EVOO, Italian seasoning, and 14° ESB in Dutch oven.
4. Place COVERED Dutch oven over extremely hot coals. Once contents are at a boil, remove cover and reduce beer to caramelized state (about 30–40 minutes).
5. Cut sheets of Hawaiian Sweet Rolls in half lengthwise. Generously lay down provolone cheese on lower half of Sweet Rolls.
6. Generously smother bread + cheese half with Philly cheesesteak from Dutch Oven. Place the other half of bread on top & let set for 2 minutes.
7. Crack open a Bent Paddle 14° ESB, tear a bun off, and enjoy!

BEER PAIRING: *Bent Paddle 14° ESB, Bent Paddle Black Ale*

Photo: Page 56, middle left & right, bottom

Ursa Minor Brewing Pizza Dough

SUBMITTED BY: BEN HUGUS, OWNER—URSA MINOR BREWING, DULUTH

This is an adapted home version of the pizza dough recipe used at Ursa Minor Brewing. It is a marriage between a traditional Italian wood-fired pizza dough and a hearty American pizza dough. Through countless trial batches, Ursa Minor found the blend provided a perfect amount of "flop" factor. You can eat it with one hand without it falling apart. Soft and delicate, yet firm and supportive, this dough is perfect for medium-sized pizzas loaded with whatever toppings your heart desires.

Dough:

- 1 1/4 c   Kyrol flour (high-gluten flour)
- 1 1/4 c   Sir Galahad flour (all-purpose artisan flour)
- 1/3 tsp   active dry yeast
- 1 tbsp   olive oil
- 3/4 c   cold water
- 1 tsp   iodized salt

Sauce:

- 1 c   canned plum tomatoes
- 1 tsp   iodized salt

MAKES ONE 12" PIZZA

1. Blend plum tomatoes and salt.
2. Preheat your oven to 500° F. (If you have a pizza stone, preheat that in the oven as well.)
3. Using a wooden spoon, mix flours, salt, and active dry yeast until well incorporated.
4. Mix the cold water and olive oil in a small bowl, then add to the flour mix, combining well. Sprinkle flour on your work surface, place pizza dough on flour and knead the dough with your hands for 10–15 minutes. (If you have a kitchen aid, mix with a dough hook on the lowest speed for 8–10 minutes. If the dough sticks to the sides of the bowl, sprinkle in a little more flour, if it is too dry add a little water. The dough should slightly stick to the bottom of the bowl.)
5. Once the dough is finished mixing/kneading, cut in half, forming two balls. Cover the dough and let sit in the refrigerator for two hours.
6. Sprinkle Kyrol flour on the counter. Press the dough around the edges, forming a circle. Stretch the dough in a 12" circle with your fingers and knuckles.
7. Dust your pizza pan with Kyrol and set dough onto the pan. Add 1/2 cup of tomato sauce and dress your pizza. (We recommend marinated kale, mushrooms, balsamic glaze and topped with ricotta out of the oven!)
8. Place in the oven and bake for 5–7 minutes or until golden brown on the edges. If you are using a pizza stone, you will have to slide the pizza on with a peel.
9. Remove from the oven and let sit for a couple minutes and add any cold ingredients.

BEER PAIRING: *Galactic Face Slap Double Hazy IPA*

Photo: Page 60, top left & right

Brewhall Pizza

SUBMITTED BY: SHAKOPEE BREWHALL, SHAKOPEE

A great pizza for the fall (Oktoberfest) season! Working with the Turtles Bar and Grill over a long-standing (3-plus-year) relationship, Shakopee Brewhall concocted a great pizza full of complementary German flavors. A Brewhall favorite and enjoyed by many!

64 oz	Shakopee Brewhall's Märzen (about 3 crowlers)
3-4	bratwursts
1	thin-crust pizza, store bought or homemade
1	white onion
4 c	ranch dressing
2 1/2 c	Dijon mustard
2	sticks of butter
4	cloves garlic, minced
2 tsp	Italian seasoning
2 tbsp	garlic salt
2 c	Parmesan cheese (optional)
	olive oil
2 c	sauerkraut
2 c	fresh mozzarella
4 c	crushed pretzels

SERVES 4–8

1. Boil 3 to 4 bratwursts in Shakopee Brewhall's Märzen. Once cooked, slice the bratwursts into 1/2" slices.
2. Caramelize one full onion and deglaze with about 2 cups of the boiling Märzen; set aside.
3. With a 3-to-1 ratio, mix ranch dressing and Dijon mustard.
4. In a small bowl, soften the butter and mix in garlic, Italian seasoning, garlic salt, and optional Parmesan to make the garlic butter.
5. Prepare a thin pizza crust and dress with garlic butter and oil.
6. Scatter 1 1/2 cups sauerkraut or more to your liking and a light amount of fresh mozzarella cheese.
7. Bake at 550° F for 10–12 minutes or until golden brown.
8. Top the pizza with a drizzle of the Dijon/Ranch blend and crushed pretzels. Enjoy!

BEER PAIRING: Märzen or a malt-forward amber or stout

Photo: Page 60, middle

Mussels de Belgique *with Pommes Frites*

SUBMITTED BY: BRIAN SCHANZENBACH, HEAD BREWER, AND RAY MINDESTROM, TAP ROOM LEAD—BLACKLIST BREWING CO., DULUTH

Brian makes this mussel recipe every time he wants to be transported to one of his favorite places, Brussels, Belgium. This recipe uses the Blacklist flagship, Or de Belgique, to put a fun spin on a traditional classic! Finish the dish off with a heaping side of Pommes Frites and you have a meal that will not disappoint!

Pommes Frites:

	russet potatoes
	vegetable oil
1/2 c	mayonnaise
1	head garlic, roasted
1 tsp	dill
1 tbsp	lemon juice
	black pepper to taste

Mussels:

2 lbs	fresh mussels
3 tbsp	unsalted butter
3 1/2 oz	fresh oyster mushrooms
1/2 c	shallots, minced
1	head garlic, minced
1/2 c	Roma tomatoes
1/2	lemon, zested
2 1/2 tbsp	lemon juice
1/2 c	Or de Belgique
1/2 c	dry white wine
	salt & pepper
	fresh chopped parsley

SERVES 4

For the Pommes Frites:

1. Peel Potatoes and cut into finger sized pieces. Soak potatoes in cold water for 1+ hours, then dry fries thoroughly with a towel.
2. In a large stockpot, bring 2 inches of oil up to 320° F. Add a handful of fries to the oil. Do not crowd the pot and stir to avoid sticking. When fries are light brown remove from the oil and let cool on a paper towel for 30 minutes. Repeat with remaining fries.
3. Bring the oil up to 375° F, and refry the fries until golden brown (around 2 minutes)—this is the key to crispy fries!
4. Place fries in a large bowl and toss with salt.
5. Create roasted garlic aioli by combining mayo, roasted garlic, dill, lemon juice, and black pepper.

For the Mussels:

1. Buy live, fresh mussels. Throw out any that have cracks, holes, or are open and do not close. Scrub the outside shell and rinse with cold water. Remove beard if present.
2. In a large pot, heat butter over a medium-high heat, add shallots and garlic, and cook until transparent.
3. Add mushrooms and tomatoes, cook for 2 minutes.
4. Add beer, wine, lemon zest and juice, and bring to a simmer.
5. Once simmering, add mussels. Cover and steam for 3 minutes, then open the lid and stir mussels. Cover again and steam until mussels open, about 2–3 minutes.
6. Season sauce with salt and pepper to taste.
7. Plate the mussels. Top with a ladle of broth, fresh parsley, and slice of lemon.

BEER PAIRING: *Or de Belgique, a Belgian style strong golden, or other light Belgian styles*

Photo: Page 60, bottom

Amber Pot Pie

SUBMITTED BY: DRU DELANGE, BREWER—WACONIA BREWING COMPANY, WACONIA

As an avid hunter, Dru tries to find different ways of utilizing the game he harvests each fall. This recipe is a favorite in the DeLange household when the weather turns cold. Although Dru uses venison, feel free to use beef/bison/elk/duck or your favorite red meat. Enjoy!

2 tbsp	butter
1	small yellow onion, diced
1 1/2 lb	venison - excess fat and silver skin removed
2 c	mushrooms, sliced
1 tsp	dried thyme
1 1/4 c	255 Amber Ale (divided)
1 tbsp	Worcestershire sauce
2 tbsp	cornstarch
1/2 c	canned corn
1/4 c	canned peas
1/2 c	canned carrots
1 tsp	salt
1 tsp	pepper
2	sheets pie crust

SERVES 6–8

1. Preheat oven to 375° F.
2. Melt the butter in a large cast iron skillet or sauté pan over medium-high heat. Add onions and venison. Cook meat until browned.
3. Once meat is browned, add mushrooms, salt, pepper, and thyme.
4. Once the mushrooms are cooked though, add 1 cup of 255 Amber Ale and the Worcestershire sauce. Bring the mixture to a boil, then reduce heat and simmer, covered, for about 5 minutes.
5. In a separate bowl, whisk the corn starch with the remaining 1/4 cup 255 Amber Ale until smooth. When the 5 minutes are up, whisk the cornstarch mixture into the meat, and simmer until the gravy reaches your desired consistency (about 5 minutes). You can add more or less cornstarch to get the desired consistency of your gravy. Thicker gravy lends to a more solid slice of pie.
6. Remove the pan from the heat and add the corn, peas, carrots, salt, and pepper. Mix well.
7. Spoon into your favorite pie crust and top it with the second crust. With a sharp knife, cut slits in the top crust to vent the pie.
8. Bake on the center rack of your oven for 35–40 minutes, or until the crust is cooked through and golden brown.

BEER PAIRING: 255 Amber Ale

Photo: Page 62, top left & right

Truth Be Told Pork Belly

SUBMITTED BY: JON ERICKSON & TREVOR ROEDIGER, HEAD BREWERS, AND SNEZANA ERICKSON, GENERAL MANAGER—ANGRY INCH BREWING, LAKEVILLE

Two brewers and a GM walk into a kitchen...while that's all true, they must Confess that the story started long before. What do you get when you mix a bunch of foodies with professional brewers? Friends who gather for the holidays to create an amazing beer-centric feast that focuses on locally-sourced, responsibly-raised ingredients and, of course, locally-brewed craft beer!

Pork Belly Marinade:

1 1/2-2 lbs	pork belly
1/4 c	soy sauce
3 tbsp	chili garlic sauce
2 tbsp	True Confessions beer
2 tsp	sesame chili oil
1 tsp	garlic, minced
1	green onion, chopped

Pear Sauce:

2 tbsp	olive oil
1-2"	piece of ginger, peeled & diced
3	thai chilies, sliced
2	garlic cloves, minced
	remaining crowler of True Confession (about 3 cups)
1/4 c	soy sauce
1/4 c	cooking wine
3 tbsp	rice wine vinegar
1	shallot, diced
2 tbsp	brown sugar
2	green onions, sliced
2	Asian pears, peeled & cubed

Optional Sides:

1/2 lb	rainbow carrots
1 1/2 lb	baby red potatoes

SERVES 4–6

1. Mix marinade ingredients together in a deep bowl or 1-gallon seal-able bag. Add Pork belly and let marinade in refrigerator while making the pear sauce.
2. Over medium heat sauté garlic, ginger, and chili peppers in olive oil, until fragrant, 2–3 minutes. Add liquids, stir to combine.
3. Peel and cube pears. Soften pears in sauce.
4. Add remaining ingredients to sauce let simmer for another 2 minutes.
5. Use an immersion blender, food processor or blender to blend the sauce and return to heat.
6. Let sauce reduce by half, be careful not to boil over. Set aside.
7. Wash and quarter baby red potatoes, par-boil for 10–15 minutes.
8. Wash and slice carrots. For softer carrots, par boil for 2–3 minutes.
9. Heat 2 tablespoons olive oil in a deep pan, preferably cast iron.
10. Cook pork belly on medium-low to medium heat until brown and crispy. Flip and repeat on the other side. Remove pork belly from pan.
11. Add par-boiled baby red potatoes, cook until crispy and golden brown. Add carrots for 2–3 minutes. Remove from pan. Slice pork belly, top with sauce, and plate with crispy potatoes and rainbow carrots.

BEER PAIRING: True Confessions or suitable Belgian Dubbel

Photo: Page 62, bottom

Coq au Bier

SUBMITTED BY: TODD DECKER, CHEF—THE FREEHOUSE, MINNEAPOLIS

This is a take on a traditional French Farmhouse dish, Coq au Vin (rooster over wine). Of course, being a brewpub, the Freehouse took the liberty of using beer instead of red wine. They chose the No. 3 English-style Brown Ale to bring some toasty, caramel, and chocolate malt sweetness to balance this hearty, savory meal.

1	whole chicken, cut into quarters
2	crowlers Freehouse No. 3 English-style Brown Ale
1/2 c	chicken stock (bone broth, or good stock)
3	sprigs fresh thyme
1 tbsp	whole grain mustard
1/4 c	sherry vinegar
1/2 c	slab bacon, diced
8-10	medium red potatoes
8-10	cippolini onions, peeled (can substitute pearl onions)
10-12	crimini mushrooms (can substitute white button)
1/4 c	canola oil
	salt & pepper to taste

SERVES 4–6

1. Preheat oven to 350° F.
2. Open a crowler of beer, measure 3 cups, set aside. (Pour remaining into a pint glass...that's for the chef!)
3. Cut chicken into quarters. Liberally season with salt and pepper.
4. On the stovetop, preheat a large heavy-bottomed pan on high heat and add enough canola oil to cover the bottom (1/4 cup). Carefully lay the chicken pieces in the pan, skin side down. Reduce heat to medium and let fat render out of skin for 3–4 minutes. Flip and cook on the second side for another 3–4 minutes. Remove chicken from the pan and put into an oven safe roasting dish.
5. Add bacon to the pan that the chicken was cooked in. Cook bacon, rendering fat, for 5 minutes.
6. Add onions, mushrooms and potatoes. Let all the vegetables cook together on high heat for 3–4 minutes, stirring to marry the flavors together.
7. Deglaze pan with 3 cups of Freehouse No. 3 beer, stock, and sherry vinegar.
8. Stir in mustard, then bring the liquid to simmer.
9. Pour the bacon, vegetables, and liquid contents into a roasting pan with the chicken quarters. Arrange everything so the chicken is at least 1/4–1/2 submerged in liquid. Place thyme sprigs on top.
10. Cover tightly with tin foil and place into the preheated oven. Cook for 2 1/2 hours.
11. Pull from the oven and check to see how tender the chicken is; a good method is to wiggle the leg bone. If you can pull it from the meat, it is done.
12. Let rest, covered, for 30 minutes before eating. Serve with a French baguette or your favorite crusty bread.

BEER PAIRING: Freehouse No. 3 English-Style Brown Ale

Photo: Page 65, top

Trails Giving Turkey

SUBMITTED BY: ADAM GRAF, HEAD BREWER—COPPER TRAIL BREWING, ALEXANDRIA

Adam created a Thanksgiving turkey feast using Copper Trail beer. A delicious glaze was made, and the bird was smoked to perfection.

Turkey & Brine (adjust quantities for smaller or larger bird):

- 1 — 10-lb turkey
- 6 c — water
- 6 c — Black Betty (or other oak-aged porter)
- 4 — whole cloves garlic
- 1 — orange, quartered
- 2 dozen — cranberries, smashed
- 1 tbsp — coriander
- 1 tbsp — peppercorns
- 1 tbsp — sea salt
- 1 tsp — sage
- 1 tsp — lemon sage
- 1 tsp — basil
- season salt
- pepper
- lemon pepper
- garlic, minced
- ground mustard
- rosemary

Glaze:

- 1 1/2 c — malty amber/dark beer
- 1/2 c — bourbon
- 1 c — cranberries
- 1 — orange, split
- 1/4 c — clover honey

SERVES 4–6

For Turkey:

1. At least 24 hours in advance, mix brine ingredients together in a pot large enough to submerge the turkey, top off with water as needed once bird is in. Let soak for 24 hours at a minimum.
2. Remove bird from brine, pat dry. Season the outside of the bird with season salt, pepper, lemon pepper, minced garlic, ground mustard, and rosemary.
3. Put either in the oven, or step up your game on a Big Green Egg, at 250° F, for 20–25 minutes per pound. With about 1 hour remaining, start brushing on the glaze (see below) every 10–15 minutes until bird is finished.
4. The bird is done when internal temperature reaches 165° F.

For the Glaze:

1. Simmer almost the full can of beer on medium heat for about 20 minutes, until the beer is reduced. Then add the bourbon. If you are brave enough, flambé for some extra character. (Be safe about burning alcohol.)
2. Add the cranberries and the orange. Reduce heat to a simmer, for another 20 minutes, crushing the cranberries once they are soft. Take a sip of the remaining beer, then recycle to be kind to the environment.
3. After the mixture has simmered, strain into another pot. Add the honey and simmer for 10 minutes, stirring so that it doesn't burn. Let cool.

BEER PAIRING: Copper Trail Nuttin Better (Nut Brown Ale), Black Betty (Oaked Bourbon Porter), or Lucky Red (Irish Red Ale), or anything rich, malty, sweet, and darker

Photo: Page 65, bottom

Wee Heavy Creme Brulee

SUBMITTED BY: NICOLE GREENWELL, TAPROOM MANAGER—10K BREWING, ANOKA

Nicole is a culinary genius and her favorite dessert to make is creme brulee. Nicole took 10K Brewing's Scottish ale, Wee Heavy, and infused it into this fancy dessert.

3/4 c	heavy whipping cream
3/4 c	Wee Heavy beer
5	egg yolks
1/2 c	sugar, plus 1/4 c
1 tbsp	vanilla extract

Special Equipment:
- Ceramic Ramekins
- Mesh Strainer
- Culinary Torch

SERVES 8

1. Preheat the oven to 325° F.
2. Put the cream and beer in a sauce pan over medium heat. Cook just until its bubbly around the edges, but not boiling. Remove from heat, cover, and allow to cool for about 15 minutes.
3. In a bowl, combine the egg yolks, vanilla, and 1/2 cup of sugar. Whisk until frothy, about 3 minutes. While continuing to whisk, slowly add the cooled cream mixture until well combined.
4. Put 8 ceramic ramekins in a baking dish, filling the baking dish with about 1 inch of water. Pour your custard through a mesh strainer into ramekins.
5. Cover the baking dish with aluminum foil and bake for 40–45 minutes or until the edges are set and the middle is still slightly wobbly.
6. Remove from oven and allow to cool, at room temp, in the water filled baking dish for 30 minutes. Transfer to a plate and allow to chill and set in the fridge for 4 hours.
7. Right before serving, cover the top of your set custard with an even, thin layer of sugar (about 1/2–1 teaspoon). Run a culinary torch over your sugar slowly, until it melts and turns an amber color. Cooking tip: Don't torch the sugar until you are ready to serve. After about an hour of sitting, the sugar will start to liquefy again.

BEER PAIRING: 10K Brewing's Wee Heavy

Photo: Page 69, top

Sticky Toffee Pudding with Brave Woman Scottish Ale
Caramel Coffee Sauce

SUBMITTED BY: CATHERINE FINNIE, STEVE FINNIE, DAWN FINNIE, AND NICK NOVOTNY— LITTLE THISTLE BREWING CO., ROCHESTER

This classic UK Sticky Toffee Pudding (STP) dessert is a masterful collaboration between the Finnie Clan and Nick. With the STP recipe hailing from Scotland, and the baking and sauce creation from Rochester, this dessert is rich, sweet, and a nice scran! This dessert is traditionally steamed in a pudding tin but has been adapted here to be baked in a muffin pan to create twelve individual portions.

Cake (aka pudding):

1 1/4 c	dates, roughly chopped
3/4 c	boiling water
1 tsp	baking soda
5 tbsp	unsalted butter
2 tbsp	molasses (or black treacle)
1/4 c	dark brown sugar, packed
1 tsp	vanilla
2	large eggs
1 1/4 c	all-purpose flour
2 tsp	baking powder

Brave Woman Caramel Coffee Sauce:

1 c	Brave Woman Scottish Ale
1/2 c	cold brew coffee
1 tbsp	unsalted butter
1 c	dark brown sugar, packed
pinch	salt

MAKES 12

1. Preheat the oven to 325° F. Grease and flour 12 muffin tins.
2. Put the chopped dates, boiling water and baking soda into a bowl, stir and let stand for 10 minutes.
3. Cream the butter, molasses, and vanilla together with a mixer until well mixed. Add the brown sugar and mix again. Beat in one egg, then scrape down the sides. Do the same with the other egg.
4. Beating more gently, add the flour and baking powder until batter is smooth and thick.
5. Using a fork, stir the soaked dates, mashing dates a little, then add dates and liquid to batter.
6. Pour and scrape batter into your prepared muffin tins and bake for 20 minutes, or until a cake tester comes out clean.
7. Combine sauce ingredients in pan. Bring to a boil to dissolve butter and sugar. Reduce to designed thickness. Enjoy the remainder of the Brave Woman Scottish Ale while sauce thickens.
8. Serve individual portions warm with sauce.

BEER PAIRING: Brave Woman Scottish Ale

Photo: Page 69, right

Peanut Butter Stout Pudding

SUBMITTED BY: RACHELLE DONALDSON, HEAD CHEF, GROOVY GRUB FOOD TRUCK WITH REVELATION ALE WORKS, HALLOCK

Peanut butter, chocolate, excellent craft beer, and whipped cream...these are a few of our favorite things! Enjoy them all with Peanut Butter Stout Pudding! You can impress your friends with this decadent pudding topped with fluffy whipped cream and a peanut butter drizzle, featuring Revelation Ale Works Peanut Butter Stout. This is a dessert they'll remember!

Pudding:

2/3 c	sugar
3 tbsp	cornstarch
1 c	heavy cream
1 c	Revelation Ale Works Peanut Butter Stout
1	large egg yolk
1/2 c	70% cocoa unsweetened chocolate
1 tbsp	butter
1/2 tsp	vanilla extract

Whipped Cream:

1 c	heavy cream
1/2 c	powdered sugar
1/2 tsp	vanilla extract
2 tbsp	Revelation Ale Works Peanut Butter Stout

Peanut Butter Drizzle:

1 tbsp	butter
2 tbsp	Revelation Ale Works Peanut Butter Stout
2 tbsp	peanut butter
1 tbsp	heavy cream

SERVES 4–6

Pudding:

1. In a medium saucepan (with heat off) whisk together sugar, cornstarch, cream, beer, and egg yolk. Whisk until well combined, then add the chocolate.
2. Bring to a boil, stirring continually over medium heat. Whisk continually for 3 minutes, then remove from heat.
3. Add the butter and vanilla, stir until well combined.
4. Pour into serving dishes, chill until set, about 2 hours.
5. When you are ready to serve, prepare toppings.

Whipped Cream:

1. Add cream and powdered sugar to a cold bowl of a stand mixer.
2. Beat on high until nice peaks form, add the stout and vanilla and beat for a bit longer.

Peanut Butter Drizzle:

1. Mix all ingredients together and heat 1 minute until blended and smooth.
2. Let cool.

BEER PAIRING: Chocolate and heavy, dark, fruited beers

Photo: Page 69, left middle

Vanilla Latte Caramel Cream

SUBMITTED BY: CHEF JIM WEIDES, CHEF AND KITCHEN MANAGER—
URBAN GROWLER BREWING COMPANY, ST. PAUL

Chef Jim incorporates UG's beer in everything he creates—batters, marinades, sauces, and desserts! Chef Jim's Vanilla Latte Caramel Cream is served on UG's desserts. Several customers have asked for pint containers of the Vanilla Latte Caramel Cream. They suggest it as a topping for ice cream, brownies, cake, pie, or dipping sauce for fruit—or enjoy a bowl solo in front of the TV.

2 cans	Urban Growler Vanilla Latte Blonde Ale
2 c	granulated sugar
1/2 c	water
2 c	heavy cream
1/4 c	butter
2 tsp	pure vanilla extract
1/2 tsp	sea salt

MAKES 3 1/2 CUPS

1. In a heavy-bottomed 2–4 quart saucepan, reduce the ale over medium heat being careful not to let it foam up and boil over. The more the ale cooks the higher you can turn up the heat, to medium-high at the most. Reduce until the ale becomes a little viscous and there is about 1/2 cup remaining. Take off the heat and reserve.

2. Add sugar and water to a heavy-bottomed 4-quart saucepan. Carefully stir to dissolve the sugar and cook over medium-high heat until the mixture begins to boil. At this point, if any sugar crystals develop on the sides of the pan wash them down using a pastry brush dipped in water. Continue to cook the sugar, carefully swirling the pan occasionally, until the large bubbles begin to subside, and the mixture begins to change color. At this point do not leave the pan unattended.

3. The mixture will begin to color more. When it reaches a rich golden caramel brown, carefully add the cream as the mixture will boil vigorously. Add the reduced ale, butter, vanilla, and salt and turn the heat down a bit. Cook the sauce until it reaches a low boil, stirring with a wire whisk until all of the caramel has dissolved on the bottom of the pan.

4. Cool the sauce completely before storing it in the refrigerator in a covered container. Let the sauce warm at room temperature when needed to serve.

BEER PAIRING: *De Lovely Porter or Vanilla Latte Blonde Ale*

Photo: Page 69, bottom left

Photo Credits

Page 10:
- **Top:** Xavier Crook
- **Bottom left & right:** Glen Bruestle

Page 12:
- **Bottom:** GLUEK BEER

Page 15:
- **Top:** Gluek's Restaurant & Bar
- **Middle left & right:** Jordan Weis
- **Bottom left & right:** Jeremy Pryes

Page 16:
- **Bottom left & right:** Marcus Paulsen

Page 19:
- **Top:** Marcus Paulsen
- **Middle left & right:** Jamie MacFarlane
- **Bottom:** David Jasper & Karlee Kanz

Page 21:
- Zola Pineles

Page 22:
- **Top:** MNCBG Staff
- **Bottom:** Tucker Gerrick

Page 26:
- **Top:** Birch's on the Lake
- **Middle, all:** Inbound BrewCo
- **Bottom:** Carl Schreiber

Page 29:
- **All photos:** Lily Altemose

Page 32:
- **Top left & right:** Shawn Taylor
- **Middle:** Mehtab Taylor
- **Bottom:** Melissa Leddy

Page 35:
- Dangerous Man Brewing Company

Page 36:
- **Top (all):** Rick Didora
- **Middle:** Christina Underkoffler
- **Bottom:** Red Wing Brewery

Page 37:
- Red Wing Brewery

Page 40:
- Kieran's Kitchen

Page 43:
- **Top left:** Jace Marti
- **Top right:** Kelly Savage
- **Bottom:** Sarah Julson

Page 46:
- Mike Krivit

Page 48:
- **Top:** Wendy Dodge
- **Bottom:** Tyler Mithuen

Page 51:
- Imminent Brewing

Page 52:
- **Top:** John Klick & John Mihajlov
- **Bottom:** Laura Meyers

Page 56:
- **Top:** MNCBG Staff
- **Middle & Bottom:** Maxwell McGruder

Page 60:
- **Top left & right:** Ashley Schwantke,
- **Middle:** Shakopee Brewhall & Turtle's Team
- **Bottom:** Ray Mindestrom & Dee Nelson

Page 62:
- **Top right:** Chrissy DeLange
- **Bottom:** Krista Reynolds

Page 65:
- **Top:** The Freehouse
- **Bottom:** Samantha Graf

Page 69:
- **Top:** Julie McMullen
- **Left middle:** RaChelle Donaldson, Tylden Kossan, Lindsey Gullickson
- **Right:** Corrie Strommen
- **Bottom left:** Kabel Lefto

Thank You

A big, hearty thank you to all of our contributors and sponsors for our first-ever Minnesota Brewers Cookbook!

It is not lost on us that our industry is full of folks with big hearts, and we are so appreciative of their continued work to help Minnesota's craft breweries grow. The following businesses sponsored the production of this cookbook and continue to support our breweries year after year.

And to MN craft beer fans—thank you for purchasing this cookbook and continuing to buy local. We wouldn't be here without you.

Flavor inspiring ingredients that will add a unique profile to any style.

Light pear, green tea, light floral notes

α-acids %:	3-5
β-acids %:	5-7.4
Total oils:	0.8-1.9

Orange, vanilla, berry, candied grape

α-acids %:	13-17
β-acids %:	5.5-6
Total oils:	2-2.5

Pineapple, pine, bright citrus

α-acids %:	13-15
β-acids %:	4-5
Total oils:	2.5-4

Lemon, tangerine, green tea, melon

α-acids %:	5-7
β-acids %:	4-6
Total oils:	1.5-2

Tropical fruit, pear, apple, melon

α-acids %:	12-14
β-acids %:	5-6
Total oils:	1.6-2.5

Orange, candied lime, fruity, floral

α-acids %:	14-17
β-acids %:	3-5
Total oils:	1.6-2.4

sbradt@hopsteiner.com | hopsteiner.com | (785) 307-4587

WE ARE THE
MN BREWERY RUNNING SERIES™ AND WE RUN FOR BEER!

Join us for 5k & 10k-ish fun run events that all start and end at local breweries. All levels are always welcome. It's not about how far or how fast you go, it's just that you GO! Run, walk, jog and celebrate at the finish line.

Our co-founders Nate Herrington and Morgan Jappe originated the Brewery Running Series here in Minneapolis, MN - organizing our first ever event at Fulton Brewery in 2012 in honor of Global Running Day.

Many years and beers later, we continue to organize over 40 events per year in MN, offer monthly Virtual Distance Challenges to keep our community moving and support our fellow beer run community with operations in 20+ US States and counting. As long as there's beer, we're running for it!

CHEERS TO YOU AND ALL OUR FRIENDS AT THE MN CRAFT BREWERS GUILD!

USE THIS CODE TO REGISTER FOR AN UPCOMING EVENT:

MNCBG20

Our mission is to **be active, have fun and give back!** A portion of all proceeds support local nonprofits.

 www.breweryrunningseries.com

100% AMERICAN MADE

Your project starts with American made stainless steel and ends with over six decades of hard-earned experience in engineering, laser cutting, forming, and welding to create simply the finest example of made in the USA craftsmanship available in the brewing industry.

Our brewery design team can help you choose equipment from our 7, 10, 15, 20 or 30 barrel brewhouse categories, or guide you through the creation of something totally custom up to 320 barrels. Manual or automated, traditional or revolutionary, Crawford Brewing Equipment is the right turnkey partner to help take your brewery project from sketch to grand opening.

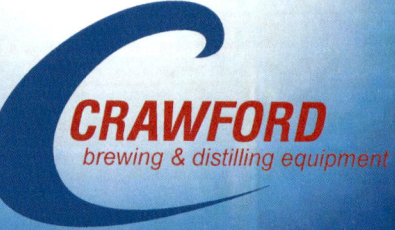

For a quote, complete our online form.
brewtanks.com | 309-788-4573

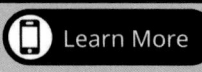

Experience the "One-Two Punch" of Alk 85 & Alk O2!

Alk 85

Heavy Duty CIP, non-foaming detergent designed as a premium Caustic cleaner for use in Breweries. Contains strong caustics, corrosion protection and chelation to emulsify and suspend particulates.

Alk O2

This industrial strength powdered detergent is loaded with oxygenated chemistry that slowly releases throughout the cleaning cycle to effectively breakdown proteins and carbohydrates left behind from the brewing process.

The Art of Beer Starts With a Clean Canvas

2020 Brewery Map

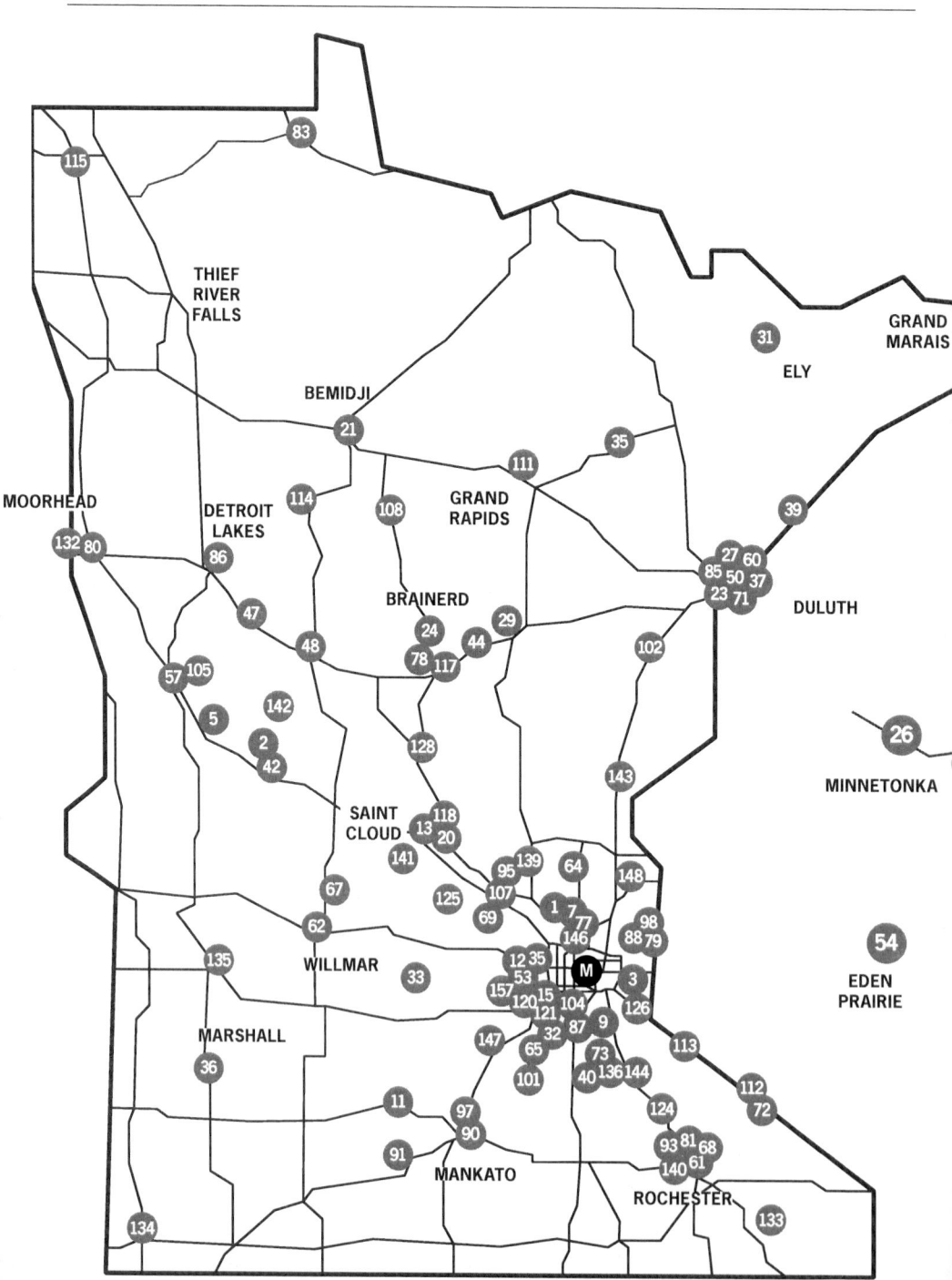

The Minnesota Craft Brewers Guild supports more than 160 breweries and brewpubs across the state. Take a look at our map and plot your next adventure to find some truly delicious beer!

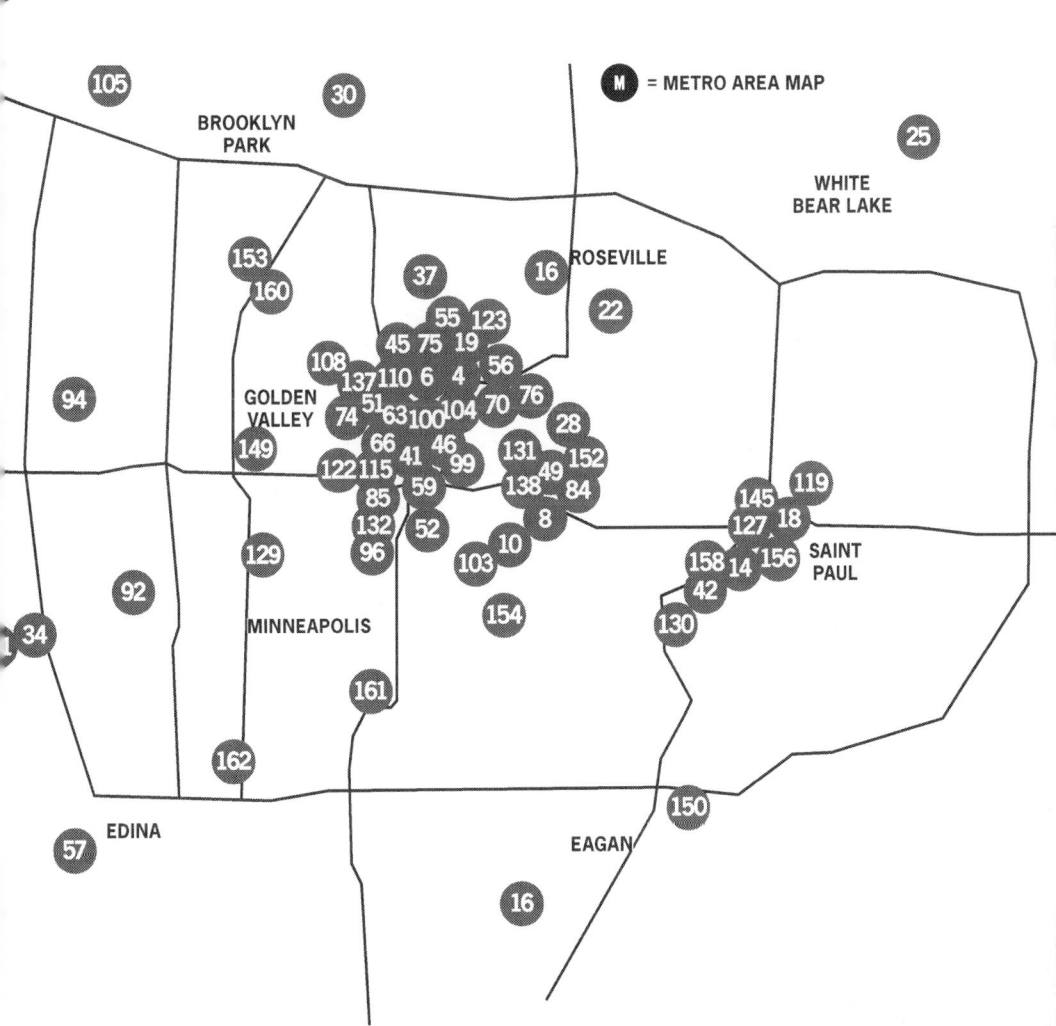

#	Brewery	#	Brewery	#	Brewery
1	10K Brewing	45	Dangerous Man Brewing Co.	89	Little Thistle Brewing
2	22 Northmen Brewing Company	46	Day Block Brewing Co.	90	LocAle Brewing Company
3	3rd Act Brewery	47	Disgruntled Brewing	91	Lost Sanity Brewing
4	612Brew	48	Drastic Measures Brewing	92	LTD Brewing Co.
5	ABC Brewing	49	Dual Citizen Brewing Company	93	LTS Brewing Company
6	Able Seedhouse & Brewery	50	Dubh Linn Restaurant & Irish Brew Pub	94	Luce Line Brewing
7	Alloy Brewing Company	51	Duluth Brewhouse	95	Lupulin Brewing Co.
8	Amanogawa Brewing Co.	52	Eastlake Craft Brewery	96	LynLake Brewery
9	Angry Inch Brewing	53	ENKI Brewing	97	Mankato Brewery
10	Arbeiter Brewing	54	Excelsior Brewing	98	Maple Island Brewing Co.
11	August Schell Brewing Co.	55	Fair State Brewing Cooperative	99	Minneapolis Town Hall Brewery
12	Back Channel Brewing Co.	56	Falling Knife Brewing Company	100	Modist Brewing
13	Bad Habit Brewing	57	Fat Pants Brewing Co.	101	Montgomery Brewing
14	Bad Weather Brewery Co.	58	Fergus Brewing Company	102	Moose Lake Brewing Co.
15	Badger Hill Brewing	59	FINNEGANS	103	Northbound Smokehouse & Brewpub
16	Bald Man Brewing	60	Fitger's Brewhouse	104	Nutmeg Brewhouse
17	Barley John's Brew Pub	61	Forager Brewery	105	Omni Brewing Co.
18	Barrel Theory Beer Company	62	Foxhole Brewhouse	106	Outstate Brewing Company
19	Bauhaus Brew Labs	63	Fulton Beer	107	Pantown Brewing
20	Beaver Island Brewing	64	Garphish Brewing Company	108	Pig Ate My Pizza Kitchen + Brewery
21	Bemidji Brewing Company	65	Giesenbräu Bier Co	109	Portage Brewing Company
22	Bent Brewstillery	66	Gluek Beer	110	Pryes Brewing Company
133	Sylvan Brewing				
134	Take 16 Brewing Co.				
135	Talking Waters Brewing Co.				
136	Tanzenwald Brewing Company				
137	The Freehouse				
138	The Lab				
139	The Nordic Brewing Company				
140	Thesis Beer Project				
141	Third Street Brewhouse				
142	Thousand Lakes Brewing Company				
143	Three Twenty Brewing Company				
144	Tilion Brewing Company				
145	Tin Whiskers Brewing Co.				
146	Torg Brewery				
147	u4ic Brewing				
148	Uncommon Loon Brewing Company				
149	Under Pressure Brewing Company				
150	Union 32 Crafthouse				
151	Unmapped Brewing Company				
152	Urban Growler Brewing Co.				
153	Utepils Brewing Co.				
154	Venn Brewing Company				

#	Brewery	#	Brewery	#	Brewery
23	Bent Paddle Brewing Company	67	Goat Ridge Brewing Co.	111	Rapids Brewing Company
24	Big Axe Brewing Company	68	Gun Flint Tavern & Brewpub	112	Reads Landing Brewing Co.
25	Big Wood Brewery	69	Hayes' Public House	113	Red Wing Brewing Company
26	Birch's Brewhouse	70	HeadFlyer Brewing	114	Revel Brewing
27	Blacklist Artisan Ales	71	Hoops Brewing	115	Revelation Ale Works
28	BlackStack Brewing	72	Hoppy Girl Brewing	116	Rock Bottom Brewery
29	Block North Brewpub	73	Imminent Brewing	117	Roundhouse Brewery
30	Blue Wolf Brewing Company	74	Inbound BrewCo	118	Rustech Brewing
31	Boathouse Brewpub	75	Indeed Brewing Company	119	Saint Paul Brewing Company
32	Boathouse Brothers Brewing	76	Insight Brewing Co.	120	Schram Haus Brewery
33	Bobbing Bobber Brewing Company	77	Invictus Brewing Co.	121	Shakopee BrewHall
34	Boom Island Brewing Company	78	Jack Pine Brewery	122	Sisyphus Brewing
35	Boomtown Brewery & Woodfire Grill	79	Joseph Wolf Brewing Co.	123	Sociable Cider Werks
36	Brau Brothers Brewing Company	80	Junkyard Brewing Company	124	South x SouthEast Brewing Company
37	Broken Clock Brewing Cooperative	81	Kinney Creek Brewing	125	Spilled Grain Brewhouse
38	Canal Park Brewing Co.	82	Klockow Brewing Company	126	Spiral Brewery
39	Castle Danger Brewery	83	Lake of the Woods Brewing Company	127	Stacked Deck Brewing
40	Chapel Brewing	84	Lake Monster Brewing	128	Starry Eyed Brewing Co.
41	Clockwerks Brewing	85	Lakes & Legends Brewing	129	Steel Toe Brewing
42	Clutch Brewing Company	86	Lakeside Tavern	130	Summit Brewing Co.
43	Copper Trail Brewing Co	87	Lakeville Brewing Co.	131	Surly Brewing Co.
44	Cuyuna Brewing Company	88	Lift Bridge Brewing Co.	132	Swing Barrel Brewing Company
				155	Voyageur Brewing Company
				156	Wabasha Brewing Company
				157	Waconia Brewing Company
				158	Waldmann Brewery & Wurstery
				159	Wayzata Brew Works
				160	Wicked Wort Brewing Company
				161	Wild Mind Artisan Ales
				162	Wooden Hill Brewing Company

Index

By primary ingredients

Apples
Peanut Butter Apple Crumble	34

Asparagus
Asparagus Risotto	13

Bacon
Happy Wife Bacon Jam	21

Beef
IGB Chili	11
Jeff Zierdt's Tater Tot Hotdish	16
Loopy Beef Sandwich	23
PB & BBQ	25
Browncoat Risotto with Beef Short Rib	27
BAMF'D Tri-Tip	30
Town Hall Shepherds Pie	31
Kriek Braised and Glazed Beef Short Ribs with Rice Lager Jasmine Rice	42
Dark Lager Beef Stacker	50
Campfire 14° ESB Philly Cheesesteak	55

Brussels Sprouts
Brussels Sprouts "Carnitas" with Beer Tomatillo Salsa	9

Carrots
Carrot Cake a la Tanzenwald	18

Chicken
Duck Fat Chicken "Carnitas" with Beer Tomatillo Salsa	9
Coq au Bier	64

Chocolate
Chocolate Stout Cake	33
Lift Bridge Stout Brownies	35
Stoneware Stout Chocolate Cake	37
Peanut Butter Stout Pudding	70

Dates
Sticky Toffee Pudding with Brave Woman Scottish Ale Caramel Coffee Sauce	68

Dessert
Carrot Cake a la Tanzenwald	18
Chocolate Stout Cake	33
Peanut Butter Apple Crumble	34
Lift Bridge Stout Brownies	35
Stoneware Stout Chocolate Cake	37
Wee Heavy Creme Brulee	67
Sticky Toffee Pudding with Brave Woman Scottish Ale Caramel Coffee Sauce	68
Peanut Butter Stout Pudding	70
Vanilla Latte Caramel Cream	71

Fish
Beer-Battered Walleye Sandwich	12
North Shore Fish Fry	17
Excelsior BrewGrub Salmon Cake Sliders	49

Marinades, Rubs, and Sauces
Beer Tomatillo Salsa	9
Happy Wife Bacon Jam	21
Loopy Beef Sandwich Chimichurri	23
Birch's Baby Back Ribs Sauce	24
PB & BBQ Sauce	25
Kriek Braised and Glazed Marinade	42
Popper Ribs Rub and Sauce	44
Spiral Into this Cheese Dip	46
Truth Be Told Pork Belly Marinade	63
Brave Woman Scottish Ale Caramel Coffee Sauce	68
Peanut Butter Drizzle	70
Vanilla Latte Caramel Cream	71

Mushrooms
Wild Mushroom Pasta	41

Mussels
Mussels de Belgique with Pommes Frites	59

Pizza
Ursa Minor Brewing Pizza Dough	57
Brewhall Pizza	58

Pork
Birch's Baby Back Ribs	24
Honey Porter Braised Short Rib Cottage Pie	28
Kieran's Rhubarb Gold Cuban Sandwich	39
Popper Ribs	44

Truth Be Told Pork Belly	63

Potatoes

Jeff Zierdt's Tater Tot Hotdish	16
Town Hall Shepherds Pie	31
Pomme Frites (with Mussels de Belgique)	59

Rice

Asparagus Risotto	13
Pragmatic Pils Lime Shrimp	14
Browncoat Risotto with Beef Short Rib	27
Kriek Braised and Glazed Beef Short Ribs with Rice Lager Jasmine Rice	42

Shrimp

Pragmatic Pils Lime Shrimp	14
Beer-Battered Shrimp	54

Snacks

Hot Dog Roller Level-Up: The Ultimate in Snack Carnage	47

Turkey

Trails Giving Turkey	66

Venison

Amber Pot Pie	61

By brewery

10K Brewing	67
Angry Inch Brewing	63
August Schell Brewing Company	41
Back Channel Brewing	33
Barley John's Brew Pub	54
Bent Paddle Brewing Company	55
Birch's on the Lake	24
Blacklist Brewing Co	59
Castle Danger Brewery	17
Copper Trail Brewing Co.	66
Dangerous Man Brewing Company	34
Eastlake Craft Brewery	9
Excelsior Brewing Company	49
FINNEGANS Brew Co	39
Forgotten Star Brewing Company	28
Fulton Brewing Company	23
Gluek Beer	12
HeadFlyer Brewing	30
Imminent Brewing	50
Inbound BrewCo	25
Inver Grove Brewing Company	11

Klockow Brewing Company	13
Lift Bridge Brewery	35
Little Thistle Brewing Co	68
LTS Brewing Co.	27
Lupulin Brewing	16
Modist Brewing Company	47
Pig Ate My Pizza Kitchen and Brewery	42
Pryes Brewing Company	14
Red Wing Brewery	37
Revelation Ale Works	70
Shakopee Brewhall	58
Spiral Brewery	46
Tanzenwald Brewing Company	18
The Freehouse	64
Three Twenty Brewing Co.	21
Town Hall Brewery	31
Urban Growler Brewing Company	71
Ursa Minor Brewing	57
Wabasha Brewing Co	44
Waconia Brewing Company	61

By beer reference

Amber Ale	58, 61
Belgian	59, 63
Blonde Ale	16, 71
Brown Ale	27, 64, 66
Cream Ale	11, 12, 17, 44
Extra Special Bitter (ESB)	55
Festbier	16
IPA	28, 44, 46, 50
IPA, Double	18
IPA, Hazy/New England	47, 49, 57
IPA, Milkshake	49
IPA, West Coast	18, 27
Kölsch	13
Kriek	42
Lager, American	9, 30
Lager, Dark	50
Dortmunder Lager	16
Lager, Rice	42
Lager, Vienna-style	17
Lambic	42
Märzen	58

Pilsner/Pilsener	9, 12, 14
Porter	21, 23, 24, 28, 30, 37, 66, 71
Porter, Peanut Butter	34
Red Ale	66
Scotch Ale	31
Scottish Ale	67, 68
Sour	9, 41, 42
Sour, Fruited	39
Stout	24, 30, 31, 33, 35, 37, 58
Stout, Coffee	23
Stout, Imperial	23, 30
Stout, Milk	24, 35
Stout, Oatmeal	23, 31
Stout, Peanut Butter	25, 70
Wild Rice Ale	54

Notes